Entrepreneur
MAGAZINE'S

DIRECT RESPONSE ADVERTISING

 **made easy**

I have always loved writing my how-to marketing articles in list format, and I love the way Roscoe Barnes has written an entire book—*Direct Response Advertising Made Easy*—using nothing but lists. It does indeed make the book easy to read and the advice easy to digest. I wish I'd thought of it! I have known Roscoe Barnes a long time, and he is a true pro. Read this book. It will help you make your advertising make more money.

—Robert W. Bly, Author of 70 books
including *The Copywriter's Handbook*

Additional Titles in Entrepreneur's MADE EASY Series

- *Business Plans Made Easy,* Third Edition by David H. Bangs, Jr.
- *Nonprofits Made Easy* by David H. Bangs, Jr.
- *Managing a Small Business Made Easy* by Martin E. Davis
- *Business Models Made Easy* by Don Debelak
- *Marketing Made Easy* by Kevin A. Epstein
- *Strategic Planning Made Easy* by Fred L. Fry, Charles R. Stoner, and Laurence G. Weinzimmer
- *Mastering Business Growth and Change Made Easy* by Jeffrey A. Hansen
- *Project Management Made Easy* by Sid Kemp
- *Advertising Without an Agency Made Easy* by Kathy J. Kobliski
- *Customer Service Made Easy* by Paul Levesque
- *Accounting and Finance for Small Business Made Easy: Secrets You Wish Your CPA Had Told You* by Robert Low
- *Meetings Made Easy: The Ultimate Fix-It Guide* by Frances Micale

DIRECT RESPONSE ADVERTISING

ADVERTISING

Entrepreneur Press and
Roscoe Barnes III

EP Entrepreneur Press

Editorial Director: Jere Calmes
Cover Design: Beth Hansen-Winter
Editorial and Production Services: CWL Publishing Enterprises, Inc., Madison,
Wisconsin, www.cwlpub.com

This publication is designed to provide accurate and authoritative information in
regard to the subject matter covered. It is sold with the understanding that the
publisher is not engaged in rendering legal, accounting, or other professional services. If legal advice or other expert assistance is required, the services of a compe-
tent professional person should be sought.

> —From a Declaration of Principles jointly adopted by
> a Committee of the American Bar Association and
> a Committee of Publishers and Associations

ISBN 1-59918-046-4

Library of Congress Cataloging-in-Publication Data

Barnes, Roscoe, 1961-
    Direct response advertising made easy / by Entrepreneur Press
      and Roscoe Barnes III.
        p. cm.
    ISBN 1-59918-046-4 (alk. paper)
    1. Advertising. I. Entrepreneur Press. II. Title.
    HF5823.B259 2006
    659.1—dc22
    Printed in Canada   2006021041

10 09 08 07 06   10 9 8 7 6 5 4 3 2 1

Contents

Contents

Introduction

What You Can Expect from This Book

*I*F YOU'D LIKE TO SEE A JUMP IN YOUR ADVERTISING RESPONSE RATES AND A boost in sales, then this book is for you.

If you'd like to improve your advertising without wasting time on thick books that are hard to follow, then this book is just what you need.

If you want to write or design an effective ad without spending a fortune on an ad agency, then this book is like money in the bank.

It doesn't matter whether you're a copywriter, entrepreneur, small or home-based business owner, marketing manager, freelance writer, or creative director, this pocket guide will help you sell more of your products and services by crafting effective advertising copy. It gives you all the essentials for good ad copy in an easy-to-use format.

This handy pocket guide is a concise, quick-reference handbook for creating ads that get results. It uses the time-tested advice in marketing to show readers how to craft effective, hard-hitting ads that generate leads, increase store traffic, make direct sales, pull orders, and boost profits. While the focus is on print ads for newspapers and magazines, the advice presented can be applied to most types of advertising, including online, direct mail, TV, and radio.

Scores of books have been written on various aspects of advertising, but unlike this book, most are not designed for quick reading—something that's needed in a busy, information-packed working environment. Many books on advertising are more suitable for a classroom than the manager of a small retail business. Large numbers of books on the topic also are more theory-oriented with little use for the person who wants immediate information that can be easily and quickly applied NOW!

Although numerous how-to resources can be viewed on the Internet, good copywriting remains a challenge. "Today, poorly written, ineffective ads, press releases, catalogs, and brochures are the norm rather than the exception," observed Robert W. Bly. "Top professionals complain that recent college graduates are ill-equipped to write the type of succinct prose necessary to awaken an interest in ideas, organizations, products, and services."

This book consists of 14 chapters, each of which is broken up with subheadlines and numbered tips, which make for scanning or easy reading—and less intimidation. As with *The Elements of Style*, the book's Table of Contents provides an easy-to-follow outline that makes it useful as a checklist.

You could say that this book is a guide for advertisers who are too busy to bother with huge manuals on the topic. It uses a fat-free presentation to give the nuts and bolts of advertising without wasting the reader's time. The book's aim is to show you—or any writer or businessperson—how to craft an effective ad. Though professionally written, the book has a personal feel that's friendly and yet serious. In this format, it serves up the critical elements for achieving advertising success. It uses a straight-forward, simple approach with colorful language, timely anecdotes, and examples. Scores of references and engaging quotes from highly respected authorities are sprinkled throughout to aid readers in further study.

The book opens with a list of the most common mistakes made by advertisers, along with suggestions for correcting the mistakes. It moves on to cover the fundamental rules for crafting effective ads and then offers a blueprint— and the tricks of the trade—for improving ads to boost response. Also included are sure-fire methods for good editing and revision, and proven ways to breathe life into weak ad copy. Throughout the text, numerous examples are given to help readers understand the ingredients of a successful ad. Appendices are added to give the reader more examples of good copy along with a helpful bibliography of recommended resources.

The format of this pocket guide makes it highly practical as a quick-reference resource. Like any good practical how-to guide, it may be read from cover to cover, by topic, or by chapter—whatever interests the reader.

Bob Hacker of The Hacker Group has said, "There are two ways to find a breakthrough: Play the rules better than anybody else; break the rules better than anybody else!" That's a good thought to keep in mind as you use this guide to breathe life into your marketing campaign.

Acknowledgments

Perhaps it is a cliché to say this, but it is true nonetheless. The writing and publication of this book would not have been possible without the help of many people. Although space will not allow for the mention of every single person, I do want to acknowledge those whose assistance was given in a very meaningful way.

Grateful acknowledgements are made first of all, to my brother, Emerson Barnes, who assisted me in a very special way. (Thanks, little brother!)

Special thanks are owed to my friends, Greg Bolyard, Stephen Reed, Rosa Mancebo, Christopher Sanders, Gershon Bai-lama Bangura, Cindy Phenicie, Tonya Orr, and Roberta Lawyer, for their support and encouragement.

Copywriter Beth Erickson of Filbert Publishing was helpful in more ways than she may realize. For that I am grateful. My friends, Alan Lane, Rod Irish and Monica Shockey, also were big supporters. (Thanks, guys!)

I also want to thank Joe Vitale for inspiring me to make the leap from journalism to marketing. His books and tapes have been a constant source of inspiration.

I am especially grateful to my agent, Bob Diforio, and my editor, Jere Calmes, along with his assistant editor, Karen Thomas. Their hard work and vision have challenged me and made this project what it ought to be. I also want to thank John Woods and the folks at CWL Publishing Enterprises, who took the manuscript and turned into the book you now hold.

Thanks to all of you for making this book a reality. Whatever success it achieves, you'll know that each of you played an important part in making it happen.

Dedication

Finally, I dedicate this book to Robert W. Bly, a mentor and inspiration to all who want to become more effective marketing communicators.

About the Author

Roscoe Barnes III is a nationally known copywriter who specializes in direct response marketing for nonprofit organizations. When he isn't busy writing copy for contributions, he writes direct mail packages and publicity copy for consumer and business-to-business markets. He also works as a publicity consultant.

Barnes has written copy for such national nonprofit clients as the World Bible Translation Center, Lautman & Co., and Good News Jail & Prison Ministry, among others. Dubbed a "renaissance writer," Barnes is one of the most versatile writers around. Since he began writing in 1982, he has established himself as an award-winning journalist, a columnist, a religious writer, a pastor and prison chaplain, an Army veteran, seminar leader, artist, book publisher, and a marketing consultant for small businesses.

He currently writes a column for *The Tidal Wave* business newsmagazine and serves as a correspondent for Publishers' Auxiliary, the official publication of the National Newspaper Association., and is a correspondent for *Publishers' Auxiliary*, the official publication of the National Newspaper Association. Barnes also is a former columnist for two national publications: *Fund Raising Management* magazine (Hoke Communications Inc.), where he wrote "Copy Thoughts"; and *Publishers' Auxiliary* (National Newspaper Association), where he wrote "Streetwise Reporting." His work has been featured in a number of popular business books: *Secrets of a Freelance Writer*, *Secrets of Successful Telephone Selling*, *The Complete Idiot's Guide to Direct Marketing*, and The AMA's (American Marketing Association) *Complete Guide to Small Business Advertising*.

Barnes is the author of eight books and training guides, the subjects of which span everything from World War II history and journalism to self-help and art. The titles include: *Secrets of a Writing Hustler* (Filbert Publishing, 2005); *The Better Letter* (Target Marketing Group, 2006); *The Guide to Effective Gospel Tract Ministry* (Church Growth Institute, 2004); *Off to War: Franklin Countians in World War II* (White Mane Publishing, 1996): *Bicentennial: Our People, Our Heritage*, (co-author, The Record Herald, 1997); *Discover Your Talent and Find Fulfillment* (McKinley & Henson, 1992); *Big Bucks from Little Sketches* (McKinley & Henson, 1993); *Scooping the Competition: How to Be FIRST in Reporting HOT Stories* (Roscoe Barnes/National Newspaper Association, 1998).

As a journalist, Barnes has worked for both military and civilian newspapers. In 1985, after working for *The Enterprise-Tocsin* (Indianola, Miss.), the

Mississippi Press Association awarded him First Place honors for "Best Investigative Reporting." In 1996, while writing for *The Record Herald* (Waynesboro, Pa.), the Pennsylvania Newspaper Publishers' Association awarded him Second Place honors for "Best News Beat Reporting." That same year, he took honorable mentions for "Best Spot News Story" and his newsroom was named "Newsroom of the Year" in a national contest sponsored by the American Publishing Company.

Barnes has published articles, book reviews, news stories, and features in trade, military, and inspirational magazines. He has published fiction in literary magazines in the United States and Germany. Barnes last worked as a full-time journalist for *Public Opinion,* a daily newspaper in Chambersburg, Pennsylvania.

In addition to The Associated Press and many state press associations, Barnes has written for: *Editor & Publisher, EurArmy, Grace in Focus, Church of God Evangel, Pentecostal Evangel, Lighted Pathway, Grit, Writers' Forum, Authorship, Writers Journal, HomeBusiness Magazine, Grace & Truth Magazine, Enrichment Journal, Pulpit Helps, Soldier, Command, BodyTalk, The Cracker Barrel Magazine, Elizabethtown Magazine,* and *At Ease.* His work has also appeared on the pages of *The Washington Post, Current Thoughts & Trends, The Patriot News* (Harrisburg, Pa.), and a number of other newspapers and magazines.

Barnes is pursuing a Ph.D. through the University of Pretoria, South Africa. He has completed graduate work with Boston University and holds a Master of Arts degree from Lutheran Theological Seminary (Gettysburg, Pa.). He earned his Bachelor of Science and Associate of Science degrees (Cum Laude) from East Coast Bible College (Charlotte, N.C.). He is a graduate and member of the Christian Writers Guild.

A native of Indianola, Mississippi, Barnes has taught writing and communication courses for the University of Maryland (Germany) and Harrisburg (Pa.) Area Community College. He's led workshops and seminars for the Mississippi Press Association, the Pennsylvania Women's Press Association, and the New York Press Association, among other groups.

Chapter 1

The 18 Most Common Mistakes Made in Advertising:
Broken Rules That Can Hurt Response

Seabiscuit had lost the race and the reasons were given through a headline in the Pacific Daily Racing Forum:

The Headless Horseman
What Was He Thinking?
Jockey Error Costs Biscuit the Big 'Cap!

S EABISCUIT'S JOCKEY, RED POLLARD, WAS BLIND IN HIS RIGHT eye. And because of this handicap, he allowed a competing horse to slip past him—on the right—and reach the finish line first. It was a simple mistake, but it cost Seabiscuit the race—and a lot of money.

In advertising, simple mistakes are made every day that cost businesses sales and profits. Mistakes that could easily be avoided are repeated to such a degree that failure becomes the norm. Like Pollard, many advertisers ride their marketing campaigns with pride and confidence. Everything seems destined to succeed. But sooner or later, they make a mistake and lose out to the competition.

The 18 Most Common Mistakes Made in Advertising

Below is a list of the 18 most common mistakes made in advertising. This list is provided to help you steer clear of trouble spots and avoid breaking the rules that can hurt your advertising response. Let it serve as a "security checklist" for closely examining and improving your work for the best results. Take a look and see if you make any of these advertising mistakes.

Mistake #1: Your headlines do not command attention

Did you know that the change in a headline can make a difference of 10 to 1 in sales?

Did you know that the change in a headline can make a difference of 10 to 1 in sales? That's right. The headline is the most important part of an ad. It is the first thing a prospect sees when he or she looks at your ad. For this reason, it must stop them in their tracks and engage them, prompting them to read the rest of your copy.

"On the average, five times as many people read the headline as read the body copy," noted David Ogilvy in *Confessions of an Advertising Man*. "When you have written your headline, you have spent eighty cents out of your dollar. If you haven't done some selling in your headline you have wasted 80 per cent of your client's money."

Headlines that command attention are those that leap from pages and announce news, benefits, advantages, and promises to the prospects. The copy is direct and speaks with a voice of authority. It may be short or long, and printed in color or black-and-white. It may ask an intriguing question ("Do You Make These Mistakes in Hiring?"), give a strong command ("Stop Hair-Loss NOW!"), or promise a benefit ("How to Win Friends and Influence People"). In all cases, it should use emotional language and key marketing words that cause prospects to stop and read your copy.

If your headline merely beats around the bush or tips up to the prospect, it sends a clear signal that you're not very proud of what you're selling—and you are reluctant to even start talking about it. A weak headline suggests timidity and uncertainty—qualities that can hardly move a prospect to action. (See Appendices for a list of headline ideas.)

Mistake #2: You focus on the product or service being promoted—and not on the prospect

The old adage, "Sell the sizzle and not the steak," remains true in advertising. Prospects want to know what you can do for them. They want to know how your offer can help them meet their needs, solve their problems, help them achieve their goals, etc.

Veteran copywriter René Gnam underscored this point in an article for *The Direct Response Specialist* (Issue 113), saying: "Too many advertisers make the critical mistake of writing copy about themselves ... 'we are wonderful and can do all these things for you.' The prospect really doesn't care about you. Instead, tell the prospect that ... 'you will be able to do all these things once you own ...'"

Mistake #3: You focus on features instead of benefits

People are deluged with all types of advertising and their tendency is to hold on to their hard-earned money. "People aren't anxious to buy, but they are eager to obtain benefits," noted marketing guru Russ von Hoelscher in *How You Can Make a Fortune Selling Information by Mail*. Your task, then, is to instill in your prospects a craving that says, "I gotta have this." And this can only be done with copy that overflows with benefits.

Features are the facts and components of your product or service; *benefits* are what prospects gain by using your product or service. Whether you write an ad, brochure, sales letter, or TV commercial, the thing that sells your product is the benefit to the user. You could list hundreds of facts about the size of your company or how your product was prepared, but a hundred facts will not pull as well as one major benefit.

Your prospects want to know, "What will I gain from using this product? How will I benefit if I spend my money for this product?" In other words, they will respond to your offer because of anticipated benefits.

Facts and features should be used to support the sale of your product; but they don't make the sale. "Convince the buyer that he or she will be better off with your product than without it—that he or she will make more money, will save time, will elevate his or her social status, or whatever copy appeal you choose," advised Allan Smith in *Selling Arts and Crafts by Mail Order*. "Decide what the benefits are, then state them over and over."

Whether you write an ad, brochure, sales letter, or TV commercial, the thing that sells your product is the benefit to the user.

Mistake #4: You speak in generalities—and not specifics

Specificity is like magic in advertising. It answers questions and at the same time, it rings with credibility. Being specific in your copy is a sure-fire way to win readers and convert them into customers.

For the most part, the more specific you are about your products or services, the better your response. "Platitudes and generalities roll off the human understanding like water from a duck," wrote advertising pioneer Claude C. Hopkins in *Scientific Advertising*. "They leave no impression whatever."

Instead of telling prospects that your product will make them lose weight, tell them how many pounds they can lose—and when. Instead of telling them they will save money, show the exact amount they can save.

Mistake #5: You dress your copy in superlatives—and not in the details that really matter

The tendency to provide fluff over substance is not uncommon among advertisers. Beginners and veterans alike fall into this trap of self-indulgence. Instead of promoting your service as "the best," "the finest," "cutting edge," or "state-of-the-art," highlight the specific qualities that set your service apart from others. Showcase the specific ways your service can help the prospect.

A string of superlatives alone is nothing more than bragging—a real turn-off to readers. But supported with facts and benefits, superlatives are like a loaded weapon: they will trigger the desired response. Whenever you use terms that hype your service, include a fact or two that supports the hype.

Mistake #6: You avoid using long copy

Despite all the evidence to the contrary, many advertisers hold on to the myth, "People won't read long copy." Somehow, the advertisers do not recall this golden rule: "The more you tell, the more you sell."

For years it has been shown that in split-run tests, long copy outsells short copy. The late advertising giant David Ogilvy had this to say: "There is a universal belief in lay circles that people won't read long copy. Nothing could be farther from the truth.... Every advertisement should be a *complete* sales pitch for your product. It is unrealistic to assume that consumers will read a *series* of advertisements for the same product. You should shoot the works in every advertisement, on the assumption that it is the only chance you will ever have to sell your product to the reader—*now or never*."

Mistake #7: Your ad has little or no credibility

Every claim in your ad must be backed up with believable, reliable evidence. If prospects don't believe your product or service will deliver what you say it will, they're not likely to respond to your offer. Today, said copywriter Galen Stilson, "ad believability must be a constant concern of every marketer." If you over-hype or promise too much, your customer will ultimately be disappointed.

Make your ads credible by supporting your claims with statistics, testimonials, case histories, strong guarantees, and any other elements that lend proof to your copy.

In this age of skepticism and fraud, your ad must have an air of truth. When you make claims in your ad that appear to be overstated, carefully take steps to reassure your prospects. The easiest way to do this, according to publisher Allan Smith, is to simply not use such claims. "Consumers are leery of exaggerations," Smith says. "It may be to your benefit to understate in order to inject the all-important element of believability into your ad."

Mistake #8: You rely on puns and clever phrases

It's one thing to make a prospect smile or chuckle and quite another to make them respond to your offer. Cleverness has its place in communications, but in advertising, it can be self-defeating. Remember: The purpose of an ad is to SELL—and not merely to tease or trigger a laugh.

"Being cute, clever, or showing off can kill response," observed direct-response designer Ted Kikoler. In most cases, an ad is strongest when it speaks directly to your prospects and avoids the risk of making them wonder about your message.

Mistake #9: Your ad resembles the competing ads that appear in the same media

Unless your ad looks different from the others, it has only a small chance of standing out from the competition and being noticed. Study your competition and take note of the ads they're using. Then figure a way to make yours different. One way to do this is to simply do the opposite of what everyone else is doing.

In most cases, an ad is strongest when it speaks directly to your prospects and avoids the risk of making them wonder about your message.

Mistake #10: You are unclear about your offer and what you want prospects to do

It helps to begin with a clear understanding of what an offer is. A good definition was expressed by copywriter Pat Friesen in *Target Marketing* (March 1997): "Your offer is the proposition you make to your prospect or customer," she wrote. "It is what you are willing to give in exchange for a response. Your offer is an entire package of elements, not just your product or price."

Stated another way: An offer consists of the price, the product or service you're selling, as well as the action the prospect must take in order to receive the purchased item. Once you have a grasp of what your offer is, you must state it in your copy in the clearest way possible. In other words, everything hinges on clarity.

Clarity is an essential quality in all advertising. The lack of it results in confusion, prompting prospects to pass you by. "To be clear is the first duty of a writer," said Brander Matthews. "To charm and to please are graces to be acquired later." The point is that clarity is a must for good writing and once it is achieved, the ideas engaged can be stated simply and concisely with brevity, directness, and organization.

Clarity is a must for good writing and once it is achieved, the ideas engaged can be stated simply and concisely with brevity, directness, and organization.

Arthur Brisbane, veteran newspaper editor, put it this way: "See a thing clearly and describe it simply. That is the essence of good newspaper work." That is also true of advertising. Use words, images, illustrations, and ideas that are easily understood by your audience. Speak in terms that they can relate to. Drive your message home with concepts that make them nod in agreement with you. Be clear about everything mentioned in your ad. Give directions that are easy to follow. Explain with utmost clarity how you want prospects to respond to your offer.

"I see but one rule: to be clear," Stendhal said to Balzac. "If I am not clear, all my world crumbles to nothing." The same thing happens to advertising: Without clarity, it crumbles.

Mistake #11: You don't give a reason for immediate action

Prospects can be reluctant, stubborn, distracted, and in some cases, too lazy to respond to your offer. The only way to move them to immediate action is to make an offer that grabs their attention and whets their appetite. Use a special price, or a premium—one or two—that appeals to your market. Provide a FREE gift if they respond by a certain date. Offer a special discount for those who respond early or to the first 50 people who call TODAY!

Use a deadline or a penalty to strike fear in your prospects. Besides telling them what they will get if they respond immediately, show them what they will lose if they miss the deadline. Outline all the benefits they will lose if they delay.

Whatever you choose to offer, make it clear in your ad that they will only receive it if they "act NOW!" Use these suggestions to create a sense of urgency in your copy.

Whatever you choose to offer, make it clear in your ad that they will only receive it if they "act NOW!"

Mistake #12: You omit the words that command attention

Take a look at your current ad. Pick up a red marker and circle all the strong marketing words that appear throughout the ad. First, look for the two strongest words in marketing, "free" and "you." How often do they appear? Next, look for other strong words such as "how-to," "new," "guaranteed," "now," "save," "new," "loss," "pain," "bonus," "gift," etc. There are other words you could choose, but the ones listed here should give you an idea. (See Appendices for more.)

Legendary author and copywriter Ted Nicholas once said that you can get everything you want in life by saying the right words. "Certain words incite many emotions and subsequent actions," he wrote in *Magic Words that Bring You Riches*. "Words have the power to induce someone to laugh, to cry, to be kind, to be loving, to be cooperative, or to buy. Or be unkind, angry, irrational."

Mistake #13: You use jargon and technical terms that are not understood by your audience

Jargon is appropriate in some cases, particularly when you're addressing a tech-savvy audience. It shows prospects that you really do know their business field. That's good. But even then, it should be used sparingly and with caution.

As an exercise, review your ad copy and circle all the terms that are commonly used by your intended audience. How many did you find? As you know, in any profession or business field, people work on different levels. You have beginners and veterans. Consequently, words that might strike a chord with the old-timers could be lost on the newcomers—even though they're working in the same field. For this reason, it would be wise to scale back the number of technical terms and use words and images that will be clearly and immediately grasped by everyone in a particular field. This is especially vital when writing for the high-tech market.

A common tendency is to use big words that impress, rather than inform. That's a mistake. Employ words that get the job done, words that move people emotionally and intellectually—and drive them to action.

Mistake #14: You don't anticipate or answer possible objections to your offer

Whether deliberately or not, when prospects read your ad, they read with certain questions and unspoken objections. When they see a claim or promise, they instinctively look for reasons to believe you. For this reason, it's important to explain the "whys" and "hows" of your product or service. Tell why it's better, faster, safer, cheaper, etc. Tell how it can do what you claim. Then back it up with solid proof.

Anticipate your prospects' objections. Then address them one by one.

In other words, anticipate your prospects' objections. Then address them one by one. Take out all possible barriers in your copy. Make it easy for readers to follow your message without hesitation. "As a copywriter, you can't ignore objections, or hope they won't come up," wrote Katie Yeakle in *The Golden Thread Online* (Issue 106, Feb. 9, 2004). "You'll do much better if you anticipate them, mention them, and resolve them as soon as possible in your copy."

After you've completed your first draft, review each promise (or claim) and imagine what objections it may trigger. Determine how you would answer these objections. Then write the answers into the copy.

Mistake #15: Your graphic illustrations do not support, reinforce, or correlate with the thrust of your copy

It's not unusual to have tension between copywriters and graphic artists, both of whom believe their work is vital to the success of a project. The copywriter wants copy to be dominant and the artist thinks that art should rule. In some cases, you have a copywriter who wants a direct-response design, but the artist wants a design that's pretty and artistic.

Beyond those scenarios, mistakes are often made when copy and art do not work together. As a rule, art should always support copy in a response ad. "Copy sells, art supports, although art can be used effectively to draw attention to your ad," said René Gnam in an article in *The Direct Response Specialist* (Issue 91, September 1994).

Mistake #16: You don't spell out a solid guarantee

A prospect may be hooked by your headline, drawn into your copy, and be spellbound by your message. But without a strong, clear, convincing guarantee, the prospect will be less inclined to respond to your offer. "You *need* a guarantee today," said Joe Vitale in *The AMA Complete Guide to Small Business Advertising*. "Since you are not the only person in your line of business, you have to somehow outflank your competition. Having a strong guarantee is one way to do that."

The preferred guarantee is one that guarantees the quality of your product or service, or it promises a refund—with or without conditions—to anyone who is not completely satisfied with your offering.

"If you want your prospects to trust you sufficiently even to ask for more information, much less to entrust you with their hard-earned money," said Dr. Jeffrey Lant in *Cash Copy*, "then you have got to give them the clear feeling you are totally, entirely, completely and profoundly dedicated to their achieving their objectives and that you will do what is necessary—whatever is necessary—to guarantee their satisfaction."

Mistake #17: You advertise in the wrong media

The need to select the right media seems simple enough. Unfortunately, money is often wasted by eager and uninformed businesspeople who consistently use the wrong media. As if by compulsion or some unseen force, they mistakenly advertise in media that are: (1) not read or used by their targeted audience, (2) not generally used by their competition, and (3) do not yield good advertising response.

When selecting the right media, think beyond the newspaper (unless you want a general audience). Focus on trade publications, newsletters, and other niche papers that are read religiously by your audience. Examine the publications used by your competition. Consider how often their ads appear. Study the formats of the ads that appear.

When you find publications that are filled with classifieds and display ads, that's a good indication that readers regularly respond to their ads. Sometimes it may be worthwhile to try "virgin territory" by advertising in a new publication or one that's not regularly used by the competition. But try it carefully and slowly, and with appropriate testing.

Mistake #18: You advertise without testing

Testing is both a safety net and a compass: It lessens the impact of possible losses, and it provides you a sense of direction for improving strategies—and future sales.

Without tests, you have no way of knowing what works and what doesn't work with your ad campaign. You could make huge errors in judgment—or create a brilliant money-making ad—and never realize either without doing a test. Testing is both a safety net and a compass: It lessens the impact of possible losses, and it provides you a sense of direction for improving strategies—and future sales.

In her book, *Successful Direct Mail*, copywriter Liz Ferdi correctly noted that the main benefit of testing is to reduce risk and be able to forecast future results accurately. "Testing allows us to find out, at a relatively low cost, whether something new is viable and worth doing again on a larger scale," she wrote.

What should you test? The elements that matter most: large ad versus small ad, the offer, the media, the headline, the body copy, etc. (We'll discuss more on this later.)

Jay Abraham, a prominent direct-marketing consultant, once told of a case that illustrates the need for testing. Here's an excerpt:

> One of my clients, a silver and gold broker, ran a headline to announce a new and very appealing marketing breakthrough. Unfortunately, he never tested his headline (and, unluckily, the headline was boring).
>
> When I entered the picture, I first came up with 10 different headlines to test. One of them outpulled his headline by more than 500%.
>
> Instead of spending $30,000 a month to produce $1 million in sales, that same $30,000 started producing $50 million in gross sales—and, at the very least, $2.5 million in additional profits. Testing your headlines can pay handsome rewards."

Abraham concluded: "Failure to test, retest and test again is tantamount to admitting that you aren't the businessperson you should be."

Chapter 2

18 Ways to Create Copy That Induces Responses:
The Rules for Crafting Ads That Get Results

I F YOU'RE LIKE MANY ADVERTISERS, YOU SHELL OUT HUGE ADVERTISING DOL- lars each year to sell your products or services. You spend and spend, and hope for the best, only to find disappointment. In some cases, the disappointment is due to a weak offer, the wrong audience, wrong media, or some of the mistakes mentioned in Chapter 1. But in many cases, disappointment can be linked to one thing: a poorly written ad that simply doesn't work. Consequently, money is wasted, fewer products are sold, and fewer people are using your services.

How to Create Ads that Get Results

In this chapter you have a list of 18 time-tested rules for crafting an effective ad. The list covers all the essentials for writing copy that gets results. Keep in mind that a good ad should reach—at the lowest possible cost—the most people who can and will buy what you have to sell. The ad should nail your prospects' attention, sustain their interest, persuade them with facts and benefits, and compel them to act. Read on and discover how the following list of rules can make a difference in your marketing campaign.

1. Determine the purpose of your ad

"All advertisements are not run for the same purpose nor to accomplish the same ends," said Chester A. Gauss and Lucius I. Wightman in a 1927 book for the American Technical Society. "Consequently," they continued, "the purpose of the advertising should be definitely determined and some distinct aim kept in view."

The point made by Gauss and Lucius in 1927 remains true even today. In fact, it's a point that must be realized at the start of any advertising campaign. For unless you know the purpose of your ad, your venture is nothing more than an exercise in wishful thinking. Generally, an ad is designed to:

▶ Sell a product or service directly, as in mail order (or direct-response marketing).

▶ Generate leads, as in business-to-business marketing.

▶ Promote awareness, as in TV advertising of consumer products and corporate services.

▶ Encourage store traffic, as in retail businesses.

▶ Promote a worthy cause, as in a fundraising campaign for nonprofit organizations.

▶ Promote a corporate image, as in full-page ads used to position a company or brand.

Determining the purpose of your ad may seem unusually basic, but it's a necessary process—and a required starting point—for creating ads that work. In his book, *Common Sense in Advertising*, Charles F. Adams called this starting point a "period of ingestion." Drink in all the facts and information you can about the subject, he wrote, "Acquaint yourself with the purposes and objectives of the campaign."

Most advertising is placed in three categories: consumer, business-to-business, and nonprofit. In the first category, products and services are aimed at consumers and they're often sold at low prices. Consumers are both the purchaser and the end user of the product or service being sold. However, in the second category, a business is targeted and the cost of the product or service is much higher—ranging from $1,000 to millions of dollars or more. Purchasing is made for a company and not an individual. Also, business purchases often involve a two-step process in which the initial ad is used to generate leads; the leads are then followed up with a call from a salesperson or a direct-mail package. In the third category, advertising is used to raise funds for a worthy cause. No product is sold unless it is used as part of the fundraising effort.

Over the years, a number of names have been used to describe different forms of advertising. The names, for the most part, are based on the industry or audience that's being targeted and sometimes, the product or service being offered. A review of the different forms may prove helpful in determining the purpose of your own ad. Some of the most commonly used names are featured here.

- ▶ **The Industrial Ad**—focuses on a product or service used by industry in manufacturing or processing. Products include items like pumps, cranes, machinery, gears, or other items related specifically to the manufacturing business.

- ▶ **The High-Tech Ad**—promotes electronics, software, computers, and other products or services of a technical nature.

- ▶ **The Trade Ad**—targets the trade rather than the general public. Considered a subcategory of business-to-business advertising, the trade ad aims to increase sales by generating enthusiasm among the people in the distribution channels: retailers, agents, wholesalers, dealers, distributors, brokers, etc.

- ▶ **The Financial Ad**—markets financial products and services, and promotes the organizations that provide them. Banking, insurance, investments, financial planning, home equity loans, tax-free bonds, mutual funds, and other such products and services are promoted through the financial ad.

- ▶ **The Health-Care Ad**—promotes products and services related to the health-care industry. This includes the marketing of medication, medical tools, and equipment as well as medical institutions.

- ▶ **The Corporate Ad**—seeks to communicate an idea, fact, or attitude dealing with the corporation as an organization rather than a specific product, service, or product line. As opposed to generating leads and sales, the purpose of the corporate ad is branding or enhancing a corporate image by placing an idea, fact, or attitude in the mind of the reader.

Please note that what you call your ad is not important so long as you create one that fits your purpose. After you have done your homework and determined what you want to accomplish with your ad, record your findings in a notebook or diary. "Put into writing your reasons for advertising—*all* the reasons—and the results you expect the advertising to bring," noted Fred. E. Hahn in his book, *Do-It-Yourself Advertising*. "You need this list to give a sharper focus to the ads you are going to create and, probably even more important, to have a method of evaluating results."

2. Make a list of all benefits

A cardinal rule in advertising is that people, prospects, readers, viewers—all respond to ads because of specific benefits that are promised to them.

A cardinal rule in advertising is that people, prospects, readers, viewers—all respond to ads because of specific benefits that are promised to them. For this reason, benefits play an important role in all ad copy. In most cases an ad will live or die by the way it presents the benefits of the products or services being promoted. Test after test has shown that the strength of an ad is often determined by its effective mentions of benefits to the reader.

Benefits are needed for several reasons, but perhaps the most important one is that they appeal to the self-interest of your customers. The appearance of benefits in an ad serves to answer the deep-seated emotional question, "What's in it for me?" Benefits—and not features—allow you to scratch people where they itch. They enable you to get their attention and hold their interest by speaking to them at the point of their need and desires.

Defining the benefits of your offering can prove challenging and sometimes result in ads that emphasize the features of a product—and not what the product can do for the prospect. When this happens, an ad is weakened and the prospect is left to wonder.

"One of the hardest things to teach copywriters is the difference between features and benefits," wrote Denny Hatch in an article for *Target Marketing* (September 2001). "The best single definition I know is the rule from *MBA* magazine: 'People want quarter-inch holes, not quarter-inch drills.'"

In the simplest of terms, a benefit is basically what a person gains as a result of using your product or service. It gives them an advantage in achieving a certain goal or desire. A feature, on the other hand, is the vehicle or mechanisms used that make the benefits possible. Put another way, a feature is what a product is or has and a benefit is what a product does.

Before writing your ad, it's absolutely essential that you know how your offering will benefit your market. Will it save them time or money? Help them to find a job? Lose weight? Buy a home? Increase security? Whatever the benefit is—and there should be more than one—it should be highlighted and repeated throughout your ad.

An easy method for determining the benefits of your offering is to take a sheet of paper and list all of its features. Study each feature with these questions in mind: "What will this do for the customer? In what way will this feature help them? What will they gain from using this particular feature?"

Then, across from each feature, write down the specific benefit it delivers. Examples:

Feature	Benefit
Product: A book titled *The Elements of Style*	
80 pages	Quick reading, saves time
Product: Military wrist watch	
Green in color	Blends with your uniform Helps you to avoid detection on battlefield
Product: Utensils	
Hard surface of stainless steel	Allows for easy cleaning and lasting beauty

After you have completed your list, review it again and determine your most important benefits. Then on a separate sheet of paper, list all of the benefits in the order of their importance. Once you've completed this step, pull out the single most important benefit and use it to develop the headline of your ad. Use the rest of the benefits from your list to develop the body copy of your ad.

In a tight market where others are offering products and services that are similar to yours, it would help to make another list. Write down all of the features of your offering, but this time, instead of listing benefits, list the ways in which your offering is different from that of your competition. Once you determine your uniqueness, find a way to mention this in your ad.

3. Choose an outline or formula that's easy to follow

Use an outline or structure that allows you to take the prospect through what is called the "motivating sequence"—a step-by-step plan that leads to a sale. One of the most effective ways to do this is to follow the AIDA formula. AIDA is the acronym for Attention, Interest, Desire, and Action. It has been around for a long time and for good reason: It works. Revised and extended versions of it have been used, but for most advertising, AIDA in its pure form will do just fine. Let's take a closer look.

One of the most effective ways to do this is to follow the AIDA formula. AIDA is the acronym for Attention, Interest, Desire, and Action.

Attention—Headline, graphic art

This is accomplished with the headline and/or graphic illustration. In some cases, the main headline is strengthened or supported by a subhead underneath.

Interest—Lead sentence and paragraph

This is established by the first sentence under the headline and the first paragraph of the ad. The prospects are hooked and intrigued by a startling statement, the presentation of a problem, a major benefit, or an engaging question.

Desire—Validated claims, personal needs or desires

This is achieved when you provide good reasons the prospects should have what you're selling. You lead them on with testimonials, facts, statistics, endorsements, etc., that support your claim.

Action—Direct request for immediate response

This is done by simply stating in clear terms what prospects must do in order to receive what you're selling. You tell them to: "Call Now," "Order TODAY," "Send this coupon today," "Bring this coupon to the nearest dealer," "Complete the attached coupon and mail it to…," "Get the facts. Call Now!" "Don't wait. Call today!"

4. Write a compelling headline

If the headline doesn't capture attention and draw readers into the body copy of an ad, the rest of the marketing effort dies a silent death.

In several places throughout this guide, attention is given to the headline. This is justified as experienced copywriters agree that without a powerful headline, a sales message stands little chance in an increasingly competitive marketplace. If the headline doesn't capture attention and draw readers into the body copy of an ad, the rest of the marketing effort dies a silent death. "The headline is unquestionably the most important element in most advertising," according to marketing guru Jay Abraham. "Likewise—it is also the most singularly important element of any selling message 'live or recorded, in person or by phone, audio or video' your company ever uses."

Robert Boduch, author of *Great Headlines Instantly!*, wrote that "If you're not allocating a sizable percentage of your time and creative effort to your headlines, you could be losing out on a large chunk of business." The experts agree.

Copywriter David Garfinkel gives this example of a weak headline, followed by one that's compelling:

Weak: "Children who don't do well at school will have many problems later on in their lives."

Compelling: "Daddy! Daddy! I got straight A's!" he said proudly. Suddenly my son's future was looking much brighter ..."

Said Garfinkel: "The first headline states a fact but does not stir emotions in a big way. The second headline, using the same number of words (17), conveys excitement, pride, and hope for the future—and it also creates a beautiful scene in the reader's mind of a happy parent-child situation."

Below are examples of nine different types of headlines. Select one or more and revise it to fit your product or service. Then do a test to see which one pulls the most response. (For more examples, see the Appendices.)

A. Startling Statement Headline
I FIRE WRITERS!
(Norman B. Rohrer, Christian Writers Guild)

B. News Headline
HOT OFF THE PRESS!
NOW BIGGER AND BETTER THAN EVER!
(Writer's Digest Books)

C. Question Headline
DOES YOUR EDUCATION MARKETING PLAN NEED A MAKEOVER?
(MKTG Education, formerly CMG Direct)

D. Clever Headline
WHEN YOU USE **"XEROX"** THE WAY YOU USE **"ASPIRIN,"**
WE GET A HEADACHE.
(Xerox)

E. Problem Statement Headline
TUMMY ACHE OR CHEST PAIN? GIVE US A CALL....
(Community General Osteopathic Hospital)

F. Command Headline
THROW AWAY YOUR QUICKBOOKS!
(ATX/Kleinrock)

G. Benefit and Promise Headline
HOLIDAY INN® BENEFITS WILL STRETCH YOUR PER DIEM
(Holiday Inn®)

H. Testimonial Headline
"MY MOTHER ALWAYS SAID, 'IF YOU CAN'T SAY THE TRUTH, DON'T SAY ANYTHING AT ALL!'"
(Don Cestone for HOT STUFF Double X)

I. Reason-Why Headline
SEVEN REASONS WHY YOU SHOULD JOIN THE AMERICAN INSTITUTE OF AERONAUTICS AND ASTRONAUTICS (AIAA)

5. Make the lead paragraph compelling and interesting

The first paragraph of an ad can make the difference between a winning ad and a losing one. If you don't get the prospect past paragraph one, it's unlikely that you'll get them at all. Therefore, you should lead with your best foot forward by using your biggest benefit, an engaging question or a startling statement in the first sentence and paragraph below your headline. "You only have three to five seconds at most to get your prospects' attention," according to Robert Kalian, author of *Mail Order Success Secrets*. "If you don't get it in that time, you have lost 'em ... forever."

After you have used a graphic and headline to grab attention, you must use the lead paragraph of your ad to build interest.

After you have used a graphic and headline to grab attention, you must use the lead paragraph of your ad to build interest. "The purpose of every sentence in an ad—headline, subhead, or illustration—is get your reader to read the first sentence," said Joe Sugarman of JS&A. He suggested using nonintimidating first sentences of 3, 4, or 5 words. Calling this "greased shoot" copy, Sugarman said it will draw prospects in on the first sentence and they'll slide down to the last. In other words, if you force prospects to read the first sentence and paragraph, there's a much better chance they'll read the entire ad.

"Shoot your biggest gun first," advised Galen Stilson. "Don't create an ad the way you would a novel. Don't build up to the climax. Don't plan out a complex plot. Tell the reader how he or she will benefit early and often."

Here's an example from an ad that appeared in *DM News*:

6. Use a tone that's appropriate to your audience

After you've caught the attention of your prospects with your first sentence and first paragraph, you must hold their attention and draw them further into your copy. One way to do this is to use a tone or style that resonates with your audience. Another way is to write like you're having a one-on-one conversation with a friend. Use concepts, words, and illustrations that reach your prospects on both an intellectual and emotional level. Aim for clarity in all areas of your "conversation."

The tone of your ad can be expressed in any number of ways, depending on your goal and your audience. It can be:

- ▶ **Breezy and chatty.** Frequently used by retailers and may include jingles. The style is similar to real conversation, much like the messages you see in e-mails and chatrooms.

- ▶ **Serious and straightforward.** Often used in business-to-business, academic, nonprofit, medical and health, and legal ads. It also may be the preferred tone for most other ads.

- ▶ **Passionate and heartfelt.** Commonly used in fundraising and political ads.

- ▶ **Angry and confrontational.** Consistently used in political ads where support is sought for a certain cause.

- ▶ **Hurrah and hard-sell.** Regularly used in opportunity ads, get-rich-quick offers, diet and weight-loss, etc.

Dr. Luther Brock, who is dubbed "The Letter Doctor," once said he read an ace piece of advice that stated: "Plain talk, please. Plumbers won't understand if you write like a college professor—but professors will understand if it's plain to a plumber."

Agreeing with the advice, Brock challenged advertisers to really think about their prospects. "No matter who your prospects are—professors, plumbers or even politicians—plain-talk (ads) win hands down in the Sales Increasing Department," he said.

Connecting with prospects and holding their attention will sometimes require the use of colloquial expressions in your copy. Just be certain that your prospects understand the expressions. "I write the way I talk," Dr. Andrew Linick once told me. And not surprisingly, Linick's approach is the preferred way of communication by many successful copywriters. Others, like Ed Mayer, suggest you "write with the ease with which you talk." Or,

Connecting with prospects and holding their attention will sometimes require the use of colloquial expressions in your copy.

put another way by Max Ross, "Write as you would talk if you could edit what you are going to say."

"I'm not going to tell you that you should write as you talk," Ross cautioned, "because your [copy] might sound pretty weird if you did."

Think back to *The Elements of Style*, in which E.B. White advised writers to write in a way that comes easily and naturally to them. He recommended using words and phrases that come readily to hand.

Should you feel the need to use jargon, make sure it is necessary and readily understood by your audience. Use slang or even technical terms where appropriate. Communicate as if you're speaking to a single individual. Pretend you've heard some exciting news and you're dying to share it. Write with a sense of urgency, but keep it friendly and personable. Use a tone that your audience can relate to.

7. Support all claims

You may indeed have the best product or service in town, but prospects will not believe it's so just because you say it. Prospects want proof. If your offer seems too good to be true, prospects will ignore it and move on to your competition.

A good ad should answer questions and address possible oppositions your prospects may have about doing business with you. The ad should hum with credibility without watering down the sales pitch. Every part of it should have a ring of authenticity. Such elements are essential for crafting ads that persuade. Below are several ways you can lure prospects by giving them the "proof" they need to trust—and respond to—your advertising.

- ▶ **Use testimonials.** Good testimonials enhance the believability of your ads. Surprisingly, many advertisers do not take advantage of them. In the book, *The Ultimate Marketing Plan*, Dan. S. Kennedy reported that while critiquing the marketing communications of thousands of people and businesses, beginners and veterans, he found the one thing lacking in their material was the use of testimonials. The collection and heavy use of testimonials is so important, Kennedy said, that you will have a strong competitive advantage from that alone. *Note:* Testimonials are more convincing if they include a photo of the quoted person, full name, title, company, city, etc.

- ▶ **Use statistics.** Do your own research or comb periodicals for facts that support your claims. Use surveys conducted by professionals, scientists, other businesses, universities. Look for numbers that prove your case, solid data that reflect credible, objective research.

▶ **Use case histories.** Insert a note about the success of one of your customers. Show how they used your product or service to reach their goals. Give the before and after story and be sure to identify the people or companies involved.

▶ **Use a notarized statement.** Find a startling comment about your product or service and have it notarized. Show a reproduction of the notary seal right on your ad.

▶ **Use professional endorsements.** Have a physician, dentist, attorney, accountant, author, celebrity, or other high-profile person endorse your claims.

Use these suggestions to reinforce your claims so prospects will have less hesitancy about your product or service.

8. Focus on the prospects and the benefits you have to offer them

Never be accused of writing "me-copy" or "company-copy." Instead, earn a reputation for writing "client-centered" or "prospect-centered" copy. Take a cue from Maxwell Sackheim. In his book, *How to Advertise Yourself*, he tells of an experience that demonstrates the importance of putting prospects first in advertising. Take a look.

> When my office was on Madison Avenue in New York a fresh young advertising writer came to me looking for a job. I didn't think much of him but he offered to bet me $10 that he could write a full-page newspaper ad, solid type, and that I would read every word of it. That got my attention! To convince me, he showed me only the headline. It read:
>
> ### This Page Is All About Maxwell Sackheim
>
> I not only paid him the $10 bet, but I gave him the job. How could I do anything else?—particulary when he explained that under the headline he would show a recent photograph of my favorite person.

Also, keep in mind that when people respond to ads or to a particular offer, they are not actually buying products, services, or businesses—they are buying benefits, advantages, or helpful results. They are buying to improve their lives, to save money, to save time, to look younger, to grow their company, to live longer, etc. They respond because of what your product or service can help them achieve. "They buy benefits—what the product *does*—not what the product *is*," said marketing consultant Chip Chaplin.

9. Use terms and ideas that are specific and concrete

Use words that paint pictures and ideas that conjure clear images in the mind of your prospect. Strive for specific nouns. For instance, instead of referring to a "tree," say "weeping willow" or "giant oak." Instead of using "car," use "BMW" or "red Toyota." Instead of talking about a "teenager," talk about a "brown-haired 15-year-old boy." And so on.

Ad copy is easier to follow when you use specifics. If an ad used the word "box" it may conjure up a vague image in your mind. But if the words "match box" were used, you'll get a single, focused image. "Use definite, specific, concrete language," advised William Strunk Jr. "Prefer the specific to the general, the definite to the vague, the concrete to the abstract."

10. Use similes to paint pictures and add interest

A good way to improve your copy and cement an idea in the minds of your prospects is by taking a familiar concept and linking it to your product or service. A couple of approaches you might consider are:

- ▶ **The If-Then Approach.** Here, you make a comparison by writing something like, "If you enjoy having _____, you'll love having this _____." "If you ever wanted a substitute for _____, then you'll appreciate having _____."
- ▶ **The Like Approach.** Make a comparison by showing the similarities between your offer and a familiar product or service. Examples: "Using this _____ is like having a _____." "This _____ is like a _____."

11. Use anecdotes to support and illustrate your ideas

The anecdote, said author Daniel R. Williamson, is part of the "heavy artillery" that writers and reporters use to conquer reluctant readers. Although small and simple, the anecdote is an effective tool for spicing up dull writing.

As a literary device, the anecdote is a little story, an episode rather than a full-length narrative, that adds color and human interest to a news story or feature article. Often it is called an "interesting account," an engaging incident, or a story-within-a-story that makes a relevant point about your topic.

To experienced writers, it's a critical device for grabbing attention. "Anecdotes are great reader pleasers," said author Gary Provost. "They are written like fiction, often contain dialogue and reduce a large issue to a comprehensive size by making it personal."

12. Highlight key words and phrases throughout your copy

Since you're not speaking to prospects face-to-face, you cannot use gestures, voice inflection, or power points to underscore certain features or benefits. Thus, you must rely on various literary devices and graphic elements that grab attention. They are:

- ▶ Underline—<u>Use with key words, sentences, subhead</u>.
- ▶ Bold—**Use with key words, main headline, subheads, etc.**
- ▶ Italics—*Use with care. Too much makes copy hard to read.*
- ▶ Capitals—Use to highlight SPECIFIC WORDS, HEADLINES, or SUBHEADS.
- ▶ Color—Red is a stopper. It's one of the strongest colors you can use to get attention.
- ▶ Indention or centering—Works best with subheads or whole paragraphs.

Don't forget devices like starbursts, arrows, reverse type, asterisks, check marks, circles, line boxes, handwritten notes, etc. Anything that will improve your ad—and make it grab the attention of your prospects—is worth trying.

Anything that will improve your ad—and make it grab the attention of your prospects—is worth trying.

Theses devices help to ensure your prospects get your message no matter how they read your copy. Whether they start from top to bottom or from bottom to top, clockwise or counter-clockwise, they will get the gist of what you're selling. For this reason, give special care to the placement of benefits throughout your copy.

13. Use subheads to break up long copy

Although subheadlines, or "subheads" (as they're commonly called) are especially useful with long copy, they also work well with short copy. Subheads serve a number of purposes. For one thing, they break up dense copy and make an ad much easier to read. They allow you to serve your sales message in small bites that are easily digestible, instead of large hunks of information.

Subheads take away what I call the "Intimidation Factor"—it's the feeling of being overwhelmed by the appearance of too many words. It results in the prospects' feeling "This is too much to read right now."

Subheads also allow for scanning. As such, they catch the busy reader who doesn't have the time or inclination to read all your copy when they see your ad for the first time. Keep in mind that when people scan, they will see a subhead that interests them and they'll stop and read that section of your ad. If you're lucky, they'll keep reading and maybe even return to the beginning and read the entire ad. Just think, without subheads, none of this would be likely.

Subheads can also be used to highlight benefits and features. They can work as "call-outs" to draw attention to certain points about your product. Additionally, subheads can work as a visual instrument to make your ad more appealing to the eye.

The best sub-heads actually deliver something about your product or service.

The best subheads actually deliver something about your product or service. As "mini-headlines," they give descriptive information or promise a benefit about your product. They can function as teasers with only a few words like, "FREE Gift when you call!" Or they can be longer, "Tax Preparation and Tax Research software together at last … for one low price."

If you have problems coming up with ideas, take the "you" approach. Beginning this way helps you to beat any writer's block. For instance: "You get _____," "You'll make _____," "You can expect _____." Fill in the blanks and you'll have effective subheads.

Try to use them under your main headline. Then insert one between each paragraph (depending on the length of your copy).

Expert marketers agree that the strongly interested prospects will generally read every word of your ad. Those who are interested in the benefits or features of your products, but not really looking to spend any money, will often just scan the page to see if it has what they're looking for.

14. Include a strong guarantee

"It's practically an unbreakable rule in mail order that you must guarantee satisfaction or money back," wrote Julian L. Simon in *How to Start and Operate a Mail-Order Business*. I believe this is true with most other forms of advertising as well. The reason is obvious: Prospects want assurance that they have nothing to lose. When they make a purchase, they are simply buying something they want or need—and not gambling. When you guarantee the quality of your product or service, and stress they should be satisfied or get a refund, prospects feel more confident about responding to your offer.

What should a guarantee include? Consider the Direct Marketing Association's guidelines for ethical business practices. They state that a guarantee should set forth terms and conditions in full in the promotion or the promotion should state how the consumer can get a copy. It should also clearly state the name and address of the guarantor and the duration of the guarantee.

According to Herschell G. Lewis, there are four standard guarantees. In the second edition of his book, *On the Art of Writing Copy*, he provides a list and examples. You'll note that all four include a refund provision.

▶ **Guarantee 1:** We Guarantee Your Satisfaction. If for any reason you aren't happy with your purchase, bring or send it back for a 100% refund.

▶ **Guarantee 2:** We Guarantee the Quality of Everything We Sell. If you think something doesn't measure up to our description of it, bring or send it back for a 100% refund.

▶ **Guarantee 3:** We Guarantee Lowest Prices. If within thirty days of your purchase, you find the identical item advertised for less, bring or send us the ad and we'll refund the difference.

▶ **Guarantee 4:** Unconditional Thirty-Day Guarantee. At any time within thirty days, if for any reason you decide you don't want to keep what you've bought, bring or send it back undamaged for a 100% refund.

15. Use a graphic illustration that supports the thrust of your copy

Illustrations, art, photographs, and cartoons should all be used to direct the eyes of your prospects to your headline and copy. Think of your graphics as an arrow: When prospects look at it, their natural inclination should be to look in the direction in which it points.

Remember that when it comes to crafting ads that get results, art is always subordinate to copy. The long-standing rule by successful marketers is that copy should determine the art you use. Otherwise, you have the tail wagging the dog, so to speak.

Although art captures attention, illustrates, and reinforces the selling message, it is the copy that does the selling. "Most artists can make an ad prettier ... or more attractive ... or enhance the copy with graphics," said

Illustrations, art, photographs, and cartoons should all be used to direct the eyes of your prospects to your headline and copy.

25

Rene Gnam. "Most artists DO NOT know how to improve response! They studied art, not bottom-line response."

16. Make a clear call for action

After you've sold your prospects on the benefits of your product, you've got to sell the benefits of action. In the clearest terms possible, you must speak directly to them and tell them exactly what they need to do to receive your offer.

It may surprise us to know how many sales are lost, not because the prospects didn't intend to buy, but because they were not convinced they should buy NOW. It goes without saying that every ad needs a strong call to action. This imperative element of your copy should include all of the ways your prospects can respond. You can strengthen it with a sense of urgency by writing, "HURRY!" "Don't wait! ... Don't delay!" "Call TODAY!" etc.

17. Include all contact information with codes where applicable

Give them multiple options for making contact with your company and use a code in order to track response.

Make it easy for prospects to reach you, whether they have questions or they simply want to place an order. Give them multiple options for making contact with your company and use a code in order to track response.

"All response ads must be coded," said René Gnam in a column for *The Direct Response Specialist* (Issue 91, September 1994). "It's the only way you'll be able to track the effectiveness of each publication, each issue of each publication, and the test ads you run. Plus, coding allows you to track backend business by publication, issue and test ad."

Include all relevant contact information: street address or post office box, e-mail address, web site, phone number, and fax. If you use a coupon, place the contact information in both the coupon and in the body copy (near the end) of the ad. That way, if the coupon is cut off and mailed, the prospects still have your contact information available.

18. Edit and revise relentlessly

The best writing is that which has been edited and revised: It is stripped of excess verbiage and trimmed into a fine-tuned, simple work of communication. "Complicated writing seems to come naturally," wrote Norman B. Rohrer. "Simplified writing takes a lot more work."

Let's face it: When it comes to crafting good copy, writers have to be *brutal*. "Editing hurts," said Thomas A. Noton. "One must bleed internally in order to cut his work and make it the best it can be." When it comes to being understood, persuasive, and effective in advertising, writers must be willing to sacrifice pet phrases, puffed-up adjectives, vague nouns, and other nuances to improve their work.

Kurt Vonnegut, famed author of *Slaughterhouse Five*, once said that writers should be hard on themselves. They should be ruthless, relentless, and downright brutal with their prose, stripping it of everything that doesn't matter. "Have the guts to cut," he said in *How to Use the Power of the Printed Word*. "Be merciless on yourself. If a sentence does not illuminate your subject in some new and useful way, scratch it out."

In his book, *So You Want to Be a Writer*, Carl Perrin gives some good advice on editing. He notes that whereas revising concerns itself with the broad structure of the work, editing looks at the details. Editing, he says, is where you can look at the paragraphs and sentences and make sure they flow smoothly. He advised:

▶ Be sure you have transitional words and expressions where you need them to show relationships between ideas. Look at your sentences and make sure they are all structurally correct.

▶ Check your grammar. Be sure that all your pronouns go with their antecedents correctly. Check your subjects and verbs to be sure they agree. Make sure your modification is all clear.

▶ Check your punctuation and capitalization. If you're not sure about a point in either of these areas, look it up in your reference manual. If you're not sure where to look to check those things, if you're not sure what some of the terms mean, get someone else to check your grammar for you, but eventually you're going to have to learn it yourself.

Galen Stilson suggests the use of a tape recorder. He encourages writers to record their writing and then play it back, and listen carefully. "What you're listening for," he said, "are sentences that are too long (no sentence should require more than one breath) ... any stumbling blocks to smooth copy flow ... confusing words ... awkward combinations of words or phrases ... words that are difficult to pronounce ... too much 'we' and not enough of 'you' ... possible misconceptions, misperceptions and negative connotations."

Chapter 3

9 Things You Should Know About Using Quotes:
A Few Tricks of the Trade for Improving All of Your Advertising Copy

THERE'S SOMETHING ABOUT QUOTES THAT GETS PEOPLE'S ATTENTION. Whether you lecture as a professor, write as a reporter, or tell jokes as a comedian, a good quote can make a big difference in your success. Be it funny or serious, provocative or profound, the right quote can nail the attention of your audience. It can stop them in their tracks and force them to open an envelope—or to read an ad. It can lure them into reading a letter or writing a check.

For those reasons, I invite you to rethink your views on using quotes (and quotation marks) in your advertising copy. Take a moment and see how you can use them for all they're worth.

According to marketing guru Ted Nicholas, an advertisement headline draws 28 percent more attention if quotation marks are around it. "It appears much more important because someone is being quoted. Therefore, it should be read," he said.

A Few Methods Worth Trying

Below are some practical, sensible ways to find the magic in quotes. As you will see, quotes can be used in a number of ways and for a number of reasons.

1. They work as teasers for envelopes

One obvious way to use a quote is as a teaser on an envelope. That could work with or without attribution.

Example: "I am pleased to endorse candidate Bill Shuster for Congress. I think he'll make a great Congressman because …" —Pres. George W. Bush

That quote has weight because of its attribution—the president of the United States. In such a case, it would be wise to highlight his name, making it jump off the package.

The teaser also works because of the curiosity factor. Instead of listing the reasons on the envelope, the reader is teased into opening the package to find the reasons.

Here's an example of a headline—without attribution—that would work outside an envelope: "When someone asks where you were on November 7th, will you say …"

By leaving it incomplete, you pique the reader's curiosity.

2. They work as headlines for letters

Quotes can have a dramatic impact on letters, particularly when used in big, bold type as a headline across the top of the page. The mere presence of the quotation marks suggests a single person is speaking, that someone is talking directly to *you*!

At the same time, the quote may imply that something important is being mentioned and it behooves you to see what it is.

Example: "This is the letter my chairman asked me not to write. He said people would be offended, because they wouldn't understand. Well, I disagree. And I think you will, too …"

Again, the goal is to tease and compel without giving away too much. The quotation marks around the statement will bolster your claim. They remind readers that an actual person is talking and that he or she is serious.

Quotes can have a dramatic impact on letters, particularly when used in big, bold type as a headline across the top of the page.

3. They work as dialogue in letters

Another way to use quotes effectively in a letter is through dialogue. Find a person with a problem that your business or product can solve. In brief passages in your letter, show that person interacting with another in order to receive help. Let's say you're helping the homeless and you want to demonstrate the need. You could write something like this:

> The young man was thin from hunger. His clothes were soiled and black from sleeping in the streets. He walked with a limp and was hunched over.
>
> "Can you help me?" he asked, shivering from the cold. "I hear this place can help people like me."
>
> "Well, you heard right," I said. "Come inside."
>
> He came inside and took a hot shower. He got a fresh change of clothes and a warm meal, with a hot cup of coffee. When he was done eating, he asked if he could shake my hand.
>
> "Just want to thank you," he said. "You people really do care."

You see, dialogue takes you into story-telling, giving you a powerful way to connect with readers.

4. They can improve advertisements

A good advertising headline can also be made stronger when it appears inside quotation marks.

A good advertising headline can also be made stronger when it appears inside quotation marks. Consider this one from Herman Chiropractic Center.

> "I had pain standing, sitting, doing ANYTHING!!! Then I did this ..."

Underneath that quote is a head shot of an elderly gentleman named Robert Henry. He has a big smile and is facing the camera—the reader.

No mistake about it. That quote, printed in red type, speaks directly to the people in pain. It has a personal feel and oozes with credibility.

Now, compare that headline with this one by a candidate for public office. It appears with the candidate's photo and a message—without quotation marks—that says, VOTE REPUBLICAN.

Under the headline appears: Allen S. Frantz, BOROUGH COUNCIL SECOND WARD. Then, in tiny type, he adds the following statement with quotation marks: "Keeping the Best Interests of the Borough Residents in Mind."

I'm sure Frantz had his reasons for running that advertisement. But in all honesty, it really doesn't say much. I read it and wondered who Mr. Frantz was and what he had to offer.

He could have improved the piece by choosing at least one critical thing he would do for the voters and then splashing it across the top of the advertisement as a quote. Voters need to feel he is speaking directly to them and that their concerns are being addressed directly by a real live human being. A good quote can make that happen.

5. They can spice up brochures

Begin your brochures with a powerful quote. Instead of a formal, dry statement about your business on the front cover, pick the most colorful statement you've heard—or the most startling one—and boldly place it on the cover.

Go inside the brochure and use a quote or two as testimonials. Insert them between sections of copy or at the top or bottom of the page. You could also make them stand alone on blank pages—with no other copy.

A brochure from Wilson College, called "Wilson College Commons," made excellent use of quotes. On the back cover of the brochure, at the very top, I found this quote:

> "The Commons is a significant element of our enrollment and retention program. Its first impression reflects the community aspect of our college environment. Students, prospective students and their parents recognize its importance to the Wilson family and the college experience," Robin Bernstein, Esq., Board of Trustees

When I opened the brochure, I found another quote on page two—with no other copy. Like the one on the back cover, it too, had the name of a respected person in the community, along with her photo.

6. They can work on response cards

The copywriter for Jews for Jesus made good use of a quote on the back of a response card. It's a comment by David Boyd, president of Israel College of the Bible. It reads:

> "I have seen firsthand the marvelous impact that Jews for Jesus is having in Israel. Many Israeli people are receiving Jesus as Messiah through their efforts. With creativity and compassion, they are reaching God's chosen people with His grace and mercy."

The quote is printed at the bottom, left-hand side of the page, just below Boyd's photo. It works well as an endorsement and a credible tool for stimulating response.

7. They can add color to features

Do you edit a newsletter? Write feature articles? If so, then you're a prime candidate for using quotes.

In her book, *Beginner's Guide to Writing & Selling Quality Features* (Portland, Oregon: Civetta Press, 1990), Charlotte Digregorio makes a strong case for using quotes in feature articles. Generally, she said, editors agree that a direct quote, used early in the story, helps to grab the reader's attention.

Digregorio said that direct quotes should be used in primarily three situations:

1. If someone says something in an interesting or colorful way that reveals a facet of their personality.
2. If one gives an opinion that would lose something if you put it in your own words.
3. If one says something very important that you wanted your reader to pay particular attention to.

"If a person uses comprehensible slang, don't clean up the quote," Digregorio said. "Use it, unless you feel that he didn't mean to, and that he slipped up with poor grammar.... If someone speaks in a colorful rural dialect, quote him in his style."

8. They can support claims and opinions

Today, it's not enough to simply make a bold claim in your writing, and expect people to act.

Today, it's not enough to simply make a bold claim in your writing, and expect people to act. You must support your claim. Back it up with proof, as in a powerful quote from an authority.

"There are two ways of establishing a proposition," said Abe Lincoln. "One is by trying to demonstrate it upon reason: and the other is, to show that great [people] in former times have thought so and so, and thus to pass it by the weight of pure authority."

9. They can show true professionalism

As noted before, some quotes can work without attribution. But others? They should be credited to some legitimate source.

Crediting sources adds an air of credibility to your copy. Your newsletters and feature articles don't have to mimic term papers. But depending on your subject, a quote and a reference note will suggest true professionalism. When you credit your sources, you show courtesy. You bring recognition to the sources while introducing your readers to other experts.

As you ponder the ideas presented here, keep in mind that people remember good quotes just as they remember good stories. Consider using a juicy, provocative quote for your next project. Make it jump out with bold type and eye-catching quotation marks. Only by trying and testing will you come to see the full potential of using quotes in your advertising copy.

Chapter 4

16 Ways to "Arrest" Your Prospects in Their Tracks:

The Rules for Increasing Responses— and Selling More of Your Products and Services

ARE YOU PLEASED WITH THE RESPONSE GENERATED BY YOUR ADS? Would you like to see better results? Higher response rates? It's perfectly alright for an ad to break even or simply cover its expenses. But, as the saying goes, "businesses exist to make money." Therefore, it's a good idea to tweak your ads to make them more effective. It's only through constant monitoring, testing, and tweaking that you can make your ads work harder and deliver the response you need to sell more of your products and services.

16 Ways to Boost Response

In this section, we will look at the rules for lifting response. If you know the audience you're trying to reach and you have a good product or service for this audience, then the suggestions offered here should work like magic. Let's take a look.

1. Use a simple format

Almost any ad can be made better by using a format that's easy to follow.

Use simple language, short sentences and paragraphs. Use subheads to keep the reader moving. Allow sufficient space between paragraphs and use bullets to list the major points of your offer. Such a format, when designed in easy-to-read type, will allow for scanning, while prodding the reader to take in your message.

"Simple writing has the power of acting invisibly," wrote Aesop Glim in the classic, *Copy—The Core of Advertising*. "That is its magic. The writer uses words—but the words of themselves are never seen. Only the ideas emerge."

Glim also wrote that people who write ads should hold this resolution: "We will write—not to be impressive, but—to be understood."

In regards to format or the actual layout and design of your ad, you should always keep your prospects in mind. According to Susan K. Jones, author of *Creative Strategy in Direct Marketing*, you would be wise to ask a number of important questions. For instance, she wrote:

"Ask yourself whether the layout presents the personality and tone that will appeal to your target market. Is it casual, sophisticated, elegant, family-oriented, hard-sell? Does the layout reflect the values and tastes of this target market by means of its visual images, typestyle, colors and border treatments?"

2. Use long copy where possible

The marketing director for a software company wanted to overhaul his catalog by using fewer words, more white space, and a few cartoons to liven up his pages. He designed a few sample pages and sent them to customers with a survey to test their reaction. To his surprise, most of the customers said they wanted less entertainment and more details about the products being sold. The marketing director discovered a golden rule that smart copywriters have been following for decades: Long copy sells.

Marketing consultant Chip Chapin rightly rejects the notion that people won't read long copy. "It's the non-prospects that hate long copy," he explains. "Prospects are the ones who want the information and always say, 'Give me more.' You need enough copy so the well-qualified prospect will do what you want him to do."

The more money you ask prospects to spend, the more copy you will need to convince them to make the purchase.

The more money you ask prospects to spend, the more copy you will need to convince them to make the purchase. An exception would be copy to generate leads or copy to merely promote an image. For ads designed to generate immediate sales, long copy is preferred.

"Don't' be afraid to use long copy or small print," advised John Caples. "Just be sure that your copy is interesting." After you have found your most efficient size ad, he said, you should jam your space full of copy, no matter whether it is a one-inch ad or a full-page ad.

3. Design your ad to look like an article

Some ads fail because they look like ads and thus, they fail to get attention.

Research shows that ads that look like the articles of the publications in which they appear can draw a far greater response than the ads that look like ads.

Research shows that ads that look like the articles of the publications in which they appear can draw a far greater response than the ads that look like ads. The ads to which I'm referring are called "advertorials" because they're designed to resemble "editorial matter." Legendary copywriter John Caples once reported on a test that proved an ad in the editorial format out-pulled an ad for the same product—set in a different format—by 81 percent.

The reason for this success is simple: People often do not read ads. Yet, some of these same people, who read only for editorial content, will slip up and read an ad if it looks like a published article.

Is this unusual? Of course not. This method of "fooling" prospects also happens on TV. You will agree, I think, that some infomercials look exactly like actual news programs and TV talk shows. The format arrests the viewers and pulls them in.

4. Use an engaging photograph or graphic illustration

Can your product or service be illustrated with a graphic? If so, then choose an illustration or a photograph with action. If your product solves a problem, then show the product solving that problem, or show the end results of having used the product.

If you're using a mug shot, then grab a picture with personality. Let the eyes of the subject look straight at the readers. If the subject is happy, then a smile, obviously, is in order. If frustrated or sad because of a nagging problem, then bring on the frowns and looks of bewilderment.

5. State the problem in your headline

"Your headline has only one job," wrote master copywriter Eugene Schwartz. "It should stop your prospect and compel him [or her] to read the second sentences of your ad."

One way to stop a reader is to forcefully state the problem you can solve in bold type. Here are some examples:

- ▶ "If you suffer from hair loss, Joe Weider has one word of advice ..."
- ▶ "Thinning Hair?"
- ▶ "Allergy sufferers!"
- ▶ "Wet Basement?"
- ▶ "Bad Credit?"
- ▶ "Confused by computers? Talk to us ..."

Maxwell Sackheim, the writer of the most successful ad in the history of advertising, mentioned a problem in the headline of his famous ad. He positioned it in the form of a question: **"Do You Make These Mistakes in English?"** The ad was used to sell a course in English and it ran for 40 years.

6. State your solution or your biggest benefit in your headline

Simply tell your prospects what your service or product will do for them. After all, people want to know, "What's in it for me?"

Can you help your prospects save money? Save time? Save energy? Enhance their looks? Help them find work? Help them make money? Improve their homes? Whatever you have that will solve their problems and make their life easier ... you can state it in your headline and nail their attention.

Consider these examples:

- ▶ "This phone system lets you take calls and smile—on even your worst days."
- ▶ "For official travel or even a little R&R, Holiday Inn Hotels offer you benefits."
- ▶ "New help for a common sexual problem."
- ▶ "Flonase works better than Claritin. Ask your doctor."
- ▶ "If you have a Honda, you can get what you need..."
- ▶ "Lose the fat, keep the muscle."

When I was writing an ad for my book, *Discover Your Talent and Find Fulfillment*, I asked myself: "What is the number one benefit a person can gain from reading this book?" I reviewed my list of possibilities and chose the biggest one. In the trade, this is called, "the ultimate benefit." Here's what I wrote:

Simply tell your prospects what your service or product will do for them. After all, people want to know, "What's in it for me?"

> Now you can...
> **UNLOCK YOUR HIDDEN TALENT**
> **... and Make the Money You Deserve!**
> **Discover Power, Fame and Big Success!**

Not surprisingly, the headline worked. It made the book a winner. For my book, *Big Bucks from Little Sketches*, I wrote:

> **You Can Make a Fistful of Dollars With a Few Little Sketches**
> **(Using Little or No Talent)**

This headline also worked. It arrested the right people and helped to sell several thousand copies within a two-year span. "Regardless of the product, it is the benefit the buyer will receive that prompts him or her to buy it," wrote Otto Kleppner in *Advertising Procedure*. "The life-giving spark of an ad is its promise of the special significant benefit the product will provide—a promise the product must be able to fulfill."

7. Describe your product or service in your headline

Take a look at your ad. What's the first thing you see? Is it the service you offer, or your company name?

If it's your company name, then you can use some help. Again, readers want to know, "What's in it for me?" They could care less about your name. For this reason, you can improve response by sounding off what you offer.

As I write this, I'm looking at a beautiful quarter-page ad that offers special auto services and products. Unfortunately, you wouldn't know that from the headline—or the largest element in the ad.

Here's the problem. When you look at this ad, the first thing you see is the word, "Crenshowernul." What, I dare ask, is "Crenshowernul"? To find out, you have to dig into the ad. Then you learn this term is not a product or service: It's the name of an auto repair company.

If you're having car trouble and you're looking through the newspaper for help, would you stop at "Crenshowernul," or an ad that screamed, "Auto repair. Quick service"?

Unless you're writing a corporate ad in which you want to make your name known, or you already have a well-known name, describe your service or product up front in your ad. Most readers will not take the time to find out what "Crenshowernul" is. The examples below illustrate how products or services may be announced in headlines.

- "LOANS! All Gain, No Pain."
- "Great books at a 30% discount!"
- "Fresh Golden Apples!"
- "FRESH GROUND CHUCK ... Freshly Ground in Store!"
- "Yes you can! Save up to $5,000 on a NEW 2007 Subaru!"
- "Rentals available! Call ..."
- "Tires! Tires! Tires! Call NOW!"

One thing to keep in mind is the marketing done by your competition. If you are advertising in a publication where no other product or service providers in your field are running ads, you can gain attention simply by stressing your product or service in the headline. Because there are no other ads for your type of offer, readers interested in your type of offer will be drawn to the headline.

On the other hand, if other advertisers, especially your competition, are using the same publication, you will need something special to make yours stand out from the crowd. In this case, you could use a clever headline, a graphic, a coupon, color, photograph—anything that will make you stand out. You also may stress the advantage of your offer or unique selling proposition, by clearly stating what makes you different.

8. Call your market by name

If you're walking in a crowd and someone screams out your name or title, you will probably jump and turn around to find the source of the scream. Next, you'll want to know why the person was screaming—and singling you out.

Such is what happens when you name your prospects in a headline: They stop and read on.

Take me, for instance. I'm a writer by trade. I love writing. And I love books and anything to do with publishing. When the words, "writing," "books," or "publishing" appear in a publication I'm reading, they get my attention. I stop immediately and read the ad. When I see those words, I see my name. I "hear" someone calling and singling me out.

What market are you trying to reach? Who are your prospects? Do you want their attention? Then use your headlines to call them by name. No, not by "John Doe" or "Mary Doe." But by their interests ... their needs ... their work ... or their desires.

Consider these examples of what I call "name-calling" headlines:

- ▶ "Attention: People who have high blood pressure or angina."
- ▶ "To men over 50."
- ▶ "Single mothers!"
- ▶ "Wanted: People who are overweight!"
- ▶ "People with back pain."
- ▶ "To manufacturers who want to boost productivity."
- ▶ "Parents!"

"Whether it's directed toward a reader, a viewer or a listener, an ad deals with only one person at a time," said Otto Kleppner. "If a person feels an ad is speaking directly to him or her, that person pays attention, otherwise not. ... The person's interest depends upon the degree to which the ad speaks about his or her interests, wants, goals, problems."

9. Highlight a FREE offer

The word "FREE" is still one of the most powerful words in marketing. It works like magic with all segments of society.

The word "FREE" is still one of the most powerful words in marketing. It works like magic with all segments of society. Use it often. Use it generously. Try it in headlines, on coupons, in the body of your ad, or in the closing. You can use it once in your copy or up to three or four times, depending on your offer. Just use it and see what happens.

A good way to start is by offering a bonus. The right one will lure your prospects and help you to qualify them. It also will help you to accurately measure the strength of your ads. And as far as your prospects are concerned, the right bonus can help them in any number of ways. For instance, it can be essential information that answers their questions, solves some of their problems, helps them save money, or helps them boost their profits.

In short, you and your prospects can benefit from the word "FREE." If you want an immediate response (and who doesn't?), add a "Bonus Benefit," advises Russ von Hoelscher. "People love to get a little extra for their money," he said. "If at all possible, offer a free bonus. This almost always increases results."

Here's how the free bonus offers can be highlighted:

- ▶ "Call now and receive a FREE guide that shows you ..."
- ▶ "If you respond in three days, we will rush you a FREE report on ..."
- ▶ "To receive a FREE sample ... call NOW or clip this ad and mail it to us with your business card."

Your free offer need not be an expensive item, but it should be something likely to appeal to the tastes, needs, or lifestyles of your readers. Consider some of the old favorites: FREE booklet, CD-ROM, eNewsletter, catalog, brochure, consultation, product sample, trial, cost-estimate, critique, etc.

10. Use a penalty or give a deadline with your offer

"What kind of advertising message has a chance to overcome inertias?" asked James Webb Young in *How to Become an Advertising Man*. "Only one that will arouse such fear of the delayed penalty, or such a vivid vision of the remote reward, that the emotional reactions will burn out the inertial block to action."

"Statistics won't do it, nor reasoned argument—though either or both may lend support," Webb continued. "Only the vivid portrayal of the reward or punishment in words, pictures, or both, has a chance."

Fear is a powerful motivator for persuasion. Using it in headlines, body copy, and even the close of an ad can increase sales.

Another effective way to increase your ad response is to put a deadline on your offer. For without a deadline, the prospects, in many cases, will procrastinate and never get around to responding.

"What I want you to understand now is how much is working against you when you set out to market," wrote Jeffrey Lant in *Cash Copy*. "You are not only competing with your competitors.... You are competing against: prospect sloth, human ineptitude, sufficient immediate comfort and insufficient pain, and everything else we humans exhibit that militates against taking action now."

Giving your prospects a reason to act NOW is crucial in effective marketing. "Unless pushed and compellingly motivated, [your prospects] will choose sloth over progress more times than not," Lant wrote. "Unless you give them a reason to act today, they will not act today. For if people do not do it NOW, they will not do it."

There are many ways and not a few gimmicks that will aid in arresting a prospect and compelling him or her to act immediately. However, the deadline is one of the most effective ones you may use, because it creates a sense of urgency. The deadline is like a warning to readers that unless they respond in a timely fashion, they will miss out on a good thing.

Dan S. Kennedy calls this the "intimidation technique." In his book, *The Ultimate Sales Letter*, he gives this example: "... If your response is received after our supply is exhausted, it will not be accepted and your check will be returned uncashed."

Fear is a powerful motivator for persuasion. Using it in headlines, body copy, and even the close of an ad can increase sales.

41

Kennedy's example, which is used over and over by successful copywriters, might be called the "wordy way" to give a deadline. But you can also be terse, concise, and say it bluntly, as in: "Order Now—Supplies are limited."

The "intimidation" technique you choose is not the big issue, so long as it is believable. Also, the more specific you are, the better. Consider the copy I used to create urgency for the sale of my book, *Off to War*:

> **Special Note:**
> Please get your order in **SOON**!
> Supply is **limited** and the book is moving FAST!
> All copies may be gone by Christmas.
> So order **NOW**! Get your copy in time for the holidays.

In response to the ad, a few people called and asked, "Do you have any more copies left?" "Will you save some for me?" "Can I rush over now?" The thought of "missing out" on this offer prompted readers to respond quickly; almost, it seemed, in a state of desperation.

11. Use testimonials at every opportunity

We are living in the age of skepticism, according to Herschell G. Lewis, author of *Direct Mail Copy That Sells*. He observed: "This is the Age in which nobody believes anybody, in which claims of superiority are challenged just because they're claims, in which consumers express surprise when something they buy actually performs the way it was advertised to perform."

One way is to enhance your credibility with the use of testimonials. They can be used inside your ad or as the actual ad itself.

How can you succeed in the face of skepticism? One way is to enhance your credibility with the use of testimonials. They can be used inside your ad or as the actual ad itself. Use them in headlines or in body copy. You can also use photos of satisfied customers and clients, along with their comments.

Whichever way you choose, however, be sure to get written permission from the people whose names and comments (and photos) you want to use. In choosing testimonials, you may select one of the following types:

- ▶ Glowing words from an authority.
- ▶ Rave reviews from the press.
- ▶ Breath-taking words from a user or satisfied customer.
- ▶ Praise from a celebrity.
- ▶ A case study of someone using your product or service.

A credible testimonial is one of the few proven techniques for convincing the readers that it's to their advantage to do business with you. As a third-party endorsement, it is much more convincing than manufacturers praising their own products.

Testimonials can be effective in just about any location in your copy, but they stand out more when used as a headline. "If your product offer is something that you believe will lack credibility on its own (lose weight in x amount of days, make x amount of $$$ overnight), then a testimonial headline is an effective way to instantly build believability in your offer," wrote Collin Almeida in *Ad Copy Tips* (Jan. 15, 2004). "And the best testimonial headline will be one that shows real results from a real user."

To illustrate his point, Almeida shared this headline:

> **Professional Headline Creator Took My Sales Letter's Conversion from a Sloppy 1% to a Whopping 4% Overnight— And I Can't Write to Save My Life!**

Like other experienced copywriters, Almeida believes testimonial headlines work because they allow someone else the chance to scream praise for your product. "It's an outside view from someone that's in comparison to the prospect reading the headline, Almeida said. "And with a strong testimonial … the excitement and results accomplished from the satisfied customer are immediately believed as something the prospect can expect to achieve too."

12. Strengthen your guarantee

Publisher Melvin Powers of Wilshire Book Company discovered many years ago that a strong guarantee can increase sales. For that reason, he said, he always put great emphasis on its use. Powers, a mail order pioneer, has been credited as the first marketer to offer a 365-day guarantee. His friend and colleague, the late Joe Karbo, engineered the practice of holding a responder's check for 30 days, promising to return it if the product ordered does not meet expectations, and then the check is returned. "While only a small percentage will be returned, knowing one has this guarantee is reassuring," Powers said. "It definitely increases orders."

Perhaps one key reason a guarantee can increase response to an ad is that it increases your credibility. That is true whether you market a product or service. A money-back guarantee will increase orders on just about any offer. "Especially for any service business that depends completely on customer satisfaction, feedback, and referrals to build their business," according to Ted Nicholas.

Testimonials can be effective in just about any location in your copy, but they stand out more when used as a headline.

An unconditional money-back guarantee is probably the ultimate guarantee, and therefore the most effective one you can use to improve response. The longer the guarantee period is, the more orders—and fewer returns—you will get, observed Nicholas. Here's an example:

Money-Back Guarantee

After you have the product for a full year, if for any reason you are not completely delighted, return it to us and receive a prompt and courteous refund.

Another type worth considering is the conditional guarantee. Because of the strings it generally has attached, it's a bit weaker than other types of guarantees. And it may even result in lower response rates. On the positive side, however, it can generate more qualified long-term customers.

Money-Back Guarantee

If, after trying out our program for up to one year (12 months) you have not achieved at least the minimum results described in our advertising, upon proof of completing the steps simply return the program for a prompt and courteous full refund of every penny you've invested.

Below are three examples of how strong, convincing guarantees may be crafted:

▶ **L.L. Bean** in its Christmas 1993 catalog:

Our products are guaranteed to give 100% satisfaction in every way. Return anything purchased from us if it proves otherwise. We will replace it, refund your purchase price, or credit your credit card, as you wish. We do not want you to have anything from L.L. Bean that is not completely satisfactory.

▶ **ATX/Kleinrock** in its Total Kleinrock Office self-mailer:

Total Kleinrock Office (TKO) comes with our 100% Total Guarantee: If at any time during your current subscription TKO fails to deliver fast authoritative answers to your toughest tax planning or compliance questions, just return it and we'll refund 100% of your subscription price.

▶ Brookstone:

In his book, *Direct Marketing Rules of Thumb*, Nat G. Bodian provides some of "the strongest and most effective guarantee words" you can use.

You must be delighted—or you get your money back. We sell only high-quality products, and we describe them truthfully. Each is carefully tested in actual use before acceptance for our catalog. We use these products ourselves.

They are: unconditionally guaranteed, ironclad money-back guarantee, no-risk guarantee, 100 percent satisfaction guaranteed, lifetime guarantee, double your money back, no-questions-asked guarantee.

Some other widely used, but less effective guarantees, use such favored wordings as: money-back guarantee, satisfaction guaranteed or your money back, complete refund if not satisfied.

Test a few guarantees and see how your prospects respond.

13. Tell the prospect what to do—and give multiple options for response

After you have gained the reader's attention—and told your complete story—you must call for action. Preferably immediate action. Encourage phone, e-mail, fax, or regular mail response. Tell the reader to call ... write ... contact a sales rep or dealer ... request more details ... or place an order.

"All my ads say the same thing," wrote Jeffrey Dobkin in an article for *Spare Time* magazine. "They say: call, write or come in. If a customer hasn't done any of these, the ad failed because we didn't get his or her business."

In the wake of Internet technology, many advertisers feature only a web address or URL (uniform resource locator) in their ads. However, it's best to include a URL that goes to a specific landing page where the reader can request more information, a demo, a free trial, or whatever it is you're offering. Doing so will increase response. If you simply include the URL of your web site that links to the home page, that will depress response.

In the wake of Internet technology, many advertisers feature only a web address or URL in their ads.

Indeed, nothing should be left to the reader's imagination. And the reader should not have to guess at what you want him or her to do. So be clear and direct with all of your instructions. Tell the reader where to call and where to write. If you're using a coupon, tell the reader—in no uncertain terms—to fill it out and mail it in immediately. If you're seeking payment with an order, then spell it out. Be specific and watch the increase in your response rate.

14. Use a coupon with your display advertisement

The coupon is a powerful ad trigger. It serves four purposes: (1) it grabs attention; (2) it makes it easy for the reader to respond; (3) it makes it easy for an advertiser to measure response; and (4) it tells the reader you have something to offer.

A coupon, by its very nature, suggests savings and easiness in ordering. It tells readers: "Hey, look! I have something for you! Here's how to get it!"

"Since all of your ads should do their best to involve the reader, a coupon is a sound way to pull a person into your advertisement," said Joe Vitale, a highly successful copywriter. "An ad with a coupon will get as much as six times more responses than the very same ad without a coupon! Put coupons in your ads! Everyone cuts them out."

Once you have created your coupon (and please make sure it looks like a coupon), remember to call for action. Tell the reader what to do. Add a line that says, "Clip and mail" or "Cut this out" along the dotted edge of your coupon.

Once you have created your coupon (and please make sure it looks like a coupon), remember to call for action. Tell the reader what to do.

Are you running an ad so small you don't have space for a coupon? Not to worry. You can turn your small ad into a coupon by surrounding it with a prominent dotted line. Then, as mentioned before, you should tell the reader to "Clip and mail" or "Clip and bring with you to a local dealer."

Is using coupons in print ads obsolete?

In early 2004, I had a discussion with Robert W. Bly that underscores the importance of coupons. It was published in his online newsletter, Bob Bly's Direct Response Letter (December 2003).

"Seems to me that fewer ads carry coupons these days," I wrote. "Are coupons still effective in this age of Internet technology?"

"Roscoe, you are right," Bly responded. "Coupons in ads have fallen out of fashion. But even though we live in an age of the Internet and 800 numbers, using a coupon in an ad still increases response, for two reasons. First, it gives the reader yet another (in addition to the Web and phone) reply mechanism. Second, and most important, it sends a visual signal to the reader that says: 'Hey, Bunky, this isn't a Madison Avenue image ad; this is one of those direct-response ads where you get something really good when you reply—so reply!'"

15. Choose the right media

The best ad in the world will flop in the wrong publication, where it's mistakenly aimed at the wrong audience. To increase your chance of success, you must look at your targeted prospects and determine what they need. Do they read the local newspaper? Trade magazines? Newsletters? Ezines?

The more you know about your prospects, the easier it will be to reach them through their favorite publications.

For example: If you're selling farm equipment, you wouldn't advertise in *Woman's Day* magazine. Instead, you would wisely advertise in a magazine that is read by farmers.

16. Regularly test important elements of your advertisements

Testing is an absolutely vital method for measuring the success or failure of an ad. It allows you to save money by spending it wisely at the right time—and in the right publications—to reach the right people.

By testing, you can also save yourself time and frustrations. You learn quickly what works and what doesn't work. By testing, you also learn how to improve your ads. As you may expect, the process of testing involves attention to detail and good record keeping.

"Most important of all factors for advertisers who want their copy to produce more inquires, and better ones, is the keeping of accurate records of the 'resultfulness' of each keyed advertisement," said Victor O. Schwab in *How to Write a Good Advertisement*. "Doing this systematically, diligently, and over a period, will cut down costly mistakes."

John Caples drove this point further (and even inspired David Ogilvy) in his book, *Tested Advertising Methods*. He said that in planning an advertising campaign, the first step should be to clear the decks of all opinion and theories. Then "find a scientific method" of testing the real strength of different ads and the various advertising media, such as publications, broadcasting, direct mail, etc. "When advertising results are not tested in some manner," Caples said, "it is difficult to know just what does pay best."

When a marketing director was once asked about testing an ad, he responded: "We have to do a survey first. We don't know which variables to test."

With or without a survey, the most important elements of an ad should be tested. Those elements are:

▶ The publication or medium in which the ad appears.

▶ The headline: Different words in the same headline as well as completely different headlines.

▶ The offer and price: This includes FREE information, samples or other incentives, the guarantee, deadlines, and the way the offer is actually stated.

▶ The graphic illustrations: Photographs, drawings, color, or provocative typeface and fonts for the copy.

▶ The time in which the ad is published.

Testing allows you to save money by spending it wisely at the right time—and in the right publications—to reach the right people.

Although some tests can be easily abused, it still is wise to use proper research when designing and running an ad to reach your market. Perhaps David Ogilvy said it best in his book, *Ogilvy on Advertising*: "Advertising people who ignore research are as dangerous as generals who ignore decodes of enemy signals."

Chapter 5

5 Ways to Use Trigger Words That Command Attention:
The Rules for Increasing Readership of Your Ads by Using Words That Connect with Prospects

"*THE DIFFERENCE BETWEEN THE RIGHT WORD AND THE* almost right word is the difference between lightening and a lightening bug," said Mark Twain. That's a good concept for copywriting, as the right word—whether written or spoken—can mean the difference in the success or failure of an ad campaign. "Sometimes you can change a single word and increase the pulling power of the ad," wrote John Caples. "Once I changed the word 'repair' to 'fix' and the ad pulled 20% more."

A similar report was shared by the marketing director for a small business. The director discovered the power of a single word by changing "try" to "use" in an offer for a software product. Instead of asking prospects to "try" the product for 30 days, they were asked to "use" the product. That single change brought a significant jump in sales. Indeed, words can incite emotions and subsequent actions. They have enormous power.

In this chapter I will explain how some of the most powerful words in marketing can be used to improve your ads. I call them "trigger words" because they grab attention and trigger response. They ignite feelings and involve the people you're trying to reach. Typically, trigger words will catch prospects through a good headline, pull them into your ad, and compel them to respond to your offer.

Why the Best Words Are Often Short and Simple

"Think as a wise man, but communicate in the language of the people," said William Butler Yeats, who won the Nobel Prize for literature in 1923. It may be OK to impress an audience with big words in a classroom or at a social gathering, but in advertising, you must use the words that can be understood by your audience. In most cases, "keeping it simple" is the way to go.

Claude C. Hopkins was a strong advocate of simplicity in advertising. He knew the power of simple words and he used that power in a simple, but mighty way. "My words will be simple, my sentences short," Hopkins wrote in his autobiography. "Scholars may ridicule my style. The rich and vain may laugh at the factors which I feature. But in millions of humble homes the common people will read and buy."

The words I will outline here are all short and simple. And there are a number of reasons for this. For starters, consider the newspaper. The articles in most of them are written on a seventh- or eighth-grade reading level. That means the news is more accessible—and more easily digested—than the contents of a professional journal. That shows, among other things, that advertisers and copywriters can learn much from the simple qualities of journalism. "Short words are best and the old words when short are best of all," said Winston Churchill.

The case for simple words can be made in many ways. For instance, if your house is on fire, do you want a thesis on the appearance of smoke and the ignition of flames that cause heat and the deterioration of an expensive housing unit or structure? Or would you want someone to shout, "FIRE"? If you were drowning, what word could be more useful than "HELP"?

Just as people can be saved and rescued by the utterance of short, simple words, they also can be SOLD by such words.

Just as people can be saved and rescued by the utterance of short, simple words, they also can be SOLD by such words.

In addition to being easily understood, simple words also can be easily remembered. Any counselor, salesperson, or reader of self-help materials can quote the title of Dale Carnegie's book, *How to Win Friends and Influence People*. That same title was wisely used as a headline to sell the book. What writer is there who cannot quote *The Elements of Style*? Is there a copywriter who cannot quote the title of Joe Karbo's book, *The Lazy Man's Way to Riches*? All of those titles/headlines are simple and direct—and easy to remember.

Let's take a look now at some of the simple trigger words that command attention. You will notice, by the way, that a number of strong marketing words are not included in this section. That's because they are mentioned elsewhere in this book. (See the Appendices for a more complete list.)

1. Use "this" or "these" in your copy

The word "this" is a real prodder. Use it in conversation and people will look to see what you're referring to. Use it in an ad and the same thing will happen. Why? The word is like an arrow: It is pointed and directional. It also works as a teaser. When "this" appears in a headline, readers tend to automatically look further to see what's said about "this."

"When you use the word 'this' … in your headline, you tend to create an attention-grabbing statement that will draw readers into the rest of your ad," said Joe Vitale. Suppose you're writing to smokers and you said, "This will help you kick the habit in 7 days or your money back."

Readers who see the headline will likely look closer to see what "this" is. Curious, they will read your copy to find answers. And that's what you want. You have teased them … prodded them … and triggered a desired response.

One of the most successful headlines written asked,

"Do You Make These Mistakes in English?"

People read that and wonder, "Which mistakes?" They read further to satisfy their curiosity.

Consider these examples:

▶ **"This popular fruit can cure you of chronic headaches. Guaranteed!"** If you have chronic headaches, wouldn't you read further? I would read the rest of it just to know what the fruit is—and I don't even have the problem.

▶ **"This lady can help you sell 3,000 books a month."** "Who is this lady?" I would ask. Even if I have no intention of using her services, I would read on simply to know who she is. I would act simply out of curiosity. If the body copy is good, I might be sold.

▶ **"This single plan can help you cut your mortgage payments in half!"** Wouldn't you want to know more about this plan?

As you can see, the word "this" cannot be ignored. It begs for attention.

It demands a reading. It compels prospects to check out what you have. When combined with other strong words, "this" is even stronger.

2. Use "you" in your copy

The word "you" is the next best thing to actually using a person's name. It's a sure-fire way to get attention. By using this trigger word, you make your ad copy personal, direct, friendly, and one-on-one. A key reason "you" is so effective is that it focuses on the reader—the prospect—and not the advertiser or the product.

"To be effective the advertisement must appeal to the reader's self-interest, not the advertiser's," said Courtland L. Bovee and William F. Arens in *Contemporary Advertising*. "If you want to get your message across and persuade the reader, use the 'you' attitude. Talk in terms of his or her needs, hopes, wishes and preferences and you are talking about the most interesting person in the world."

Besides being able to focus on your prospect's self-interest, the word "you" allows you to single out your prospects.

Besides being able to focus on your prospect's self-interest, the word "you" allows you to single out your prospects. Take the factory worker who needed change for a dollar. "Go to the break room," his boss told him. "Someone there may have it."

The worker, a young man who was new on the job, walked into the busy smoke-filled room with his hands in his pocket. "Anybody got change for a dollar?" he asked.

No one answered. So he walked over to a man who was munching down on a bologna sandwich. "Excuse me, sir," the worker said.

The man looked up, at which point the new worker made eye contact. "Do you have change for a dollar?"

"Aw, let me see," said the man. "Yep. Believe I do. Here you go."

That is what happens when you use the word "you." Instead of speaking to a crowd, you make eye contact and speak one-on-one. Shout "Hey!" to a crowd of moving people and the crowd may keep moving. But say, "Hey, YOU!" to an individual and that person will stop.

Ted Nicholas illustrated the use of this word in both an ad and a sales letter. He used this headline: **"You, a Millionaire Writer?"** He wasted no time in getting attention. If you're a writer who aspires to be a success, you know immediately Nicholas is talking to YOU! He's calling you out for a personal conversation.

3. Use "FREE" in your copy

The word "free" is still a magic word in marketing but it is no longer the driver; it's still a trigger word in that it gets attention, but for certain products and services, it no longer has the appeal it once had. It used to be that "free" alone would sell, but it is no longer the selling point. Instead, "free" is something that will kick the undecided prospects over the edge because many people still like to get free stuff for their efforts.

That said, I think it's important to note that "free" should be used with caution. Why? Because wrongly used, it can either cheapen an offer by lessening its perceived value, or it can drown you in unqualified leads or inquiries. The late Lee Howard said that "free" is definitely a valuable word so long as it is handled with care. "It still gets attention if you have a genuine FREE offer," he said.

Howard went on to say that getting lots of inquiries does not necessarily mean you have a good ad. "The quality of the inquiries is all important," he noted. "Are they really interested in your specific offer? Did you clearly tell them what you are offering?"

In other words, you need inquirers who are prepared to pay for what you have. If they don't have the interest in your offer or the money to purchase it, they are not the prospects you want.

To effectively use "free" to trigger a desired response, you need a legitimate free offer. It should be highlighted in your copy. Use it in your headline, in your opening paragraph, in subheads, in the close, on the coupon. Make the word stand out by enlarging it or placing it in all caps. Use a different color, such as red. You may also underline it or use italics.

To effectively use "free" to trigger a desired response, you need a legitimate free offer.

4. Use the "six honest serving-men"

If you have done any reading on journalism or poetry, then you are well acquainted with Rudyard Kipling's "six honest serving-men." He wrote:

I keep six honest serving-men
(They taught me all I knew);
Their names are What and Why and When
And How and Where and Who.

If you use one or more of the "six men" in your headline, you're bound to write some good copy. In fact, if you get stuck in writing a headline, put "How-to" in your copy and you're on your way.

The mere sight of what, why, when, how, where, and who suggests the promise of answers ... solutions ... benefits ... or something of worth to follow. Here's what Bob Stone said in *Successful Direct Marketing Methods*:

> Any beginning newspaper reporter is taught that a good story should start out by answering the main questions that go through a reader's mind—who, what, when, where, why and how. You can build an effective lead by promising to answer one of these questions and then immediately enlarging on it in your opening paragraphs.

Stone gave these examples:

- ▶ "How successful people really get ahead"
- ▶ "What it takes to survive in the executive jungle"
- ▶ "Why some people always get singled out for promotions and salary increases"

And the list goes on.

The fact that these six trigger words are strong can be seen through some of your favorite magazines. Take a look and you'll see that almost every copy has a "how-to" title featured on the cover. As I write this I'm looking at several issues of *Reader's Digest*. Here are some of the titles on the front cover:

- ▶ "What supermarkets know about you"
- ▶ "What an American girl can do"
- ▶ "Where Ol' Roy keeps his stuff"
- ▶ "When to follow a hunch"
- ▶ "How to handle mean people"
- ▶ "What your car is trying to tell you"
- ▶ "Where wealth begins"
- ▶ "When life throws a hardball"
- ▶ "Where it pays to have a great idea"
- ▶ "How the Life Saver got its hole"
- ▶ "What's so good about failure"
- ▶ "What happened to civility"

Now mind you, *Reader's Digest* is one of the most successful magazines of all time. It has millions of readers. So, if they employ the "six serving-men"—and continue to find success—why don't you put these "men" to work in your ads? Work them hard and see what response they trigger.

Note: The "six serving-men" can also help you select titles for books, chapters, newsletters, billboards, brochures, etc. For a good example of chapter titles, see Freeman F. Gosden Jr.'s book, *Direct Marketing Success*. His Table of Contents is literally filled with why's, what's, and how's.

5. Use "steps" and "ways" in your copy

The words "steps" and "ways" suggest numbers and lists with a promise.

The words "steps" and "ways" suggest numbers and lists with a promise. The words, usually preceded by a number (or bullets), get attention and pull readers into the copy. They work because they set the stage for an organized selling proposition. "If you use a specific number, it will attract curiosity and usually make the reader want to find out what they are," said Bob Stone.

Some examples are as follows:

▶ "7 Steps to Divine Healing"

▶ "15 Ways to Boost Response Rates"

▶ "17 little-known ways to improve your on-the-job performance—and one big way to make it pay off!"

▶ "5 steps to selling more of your software—starting now!"

▶ "The best way to make love to a good woman"

▶ "The right way to flirt with a shy man"

As you may have guessed, the use of numbers and lists is not limited to "steps" and "ways." You can use them with a host of other words. For example:

▶ "The Seven Habits of Highly Effective People"

▶ "The Seven Deadly Sins of Journalism"

▶ "Top 10 Signs the Government is Shrinking"

▶ "The 10 Sexual Senses"

The words highlighted here will work in most forms of advertising. It doesn't matter whether you use print, online, or different types of electronic media. These trigger words will command attention. Using them will not guarantee success, but it will increase your chances of success. Also, it means you will be relying on some of the most powerful, time-tested tools available for your marketing campaign.

Chapter 6

4 Ways to Use Trigger Phrases That Make People Act—Now!
The Rules for Calling Your Prospects to Action

THE STOCKY GRAY-HAIRED BUSINESSMAN SNEERED AS HE SLAMMED THE newspaper down on the counter.

"I don't believe this," he said, as he opened the paper and pointed to his ad. "I've been running ads for three years. I've tried different sizes ... different colors ... and large print. But the customers won't come!"

The ad was for a line of sewing machines.

After pausing for a moment, the man said he was dropping all ads in his local newspaper. He thought he'd try radio for a change. But I interrupted. I looked at his ad and immediately saw what was missing. The ad had a decent headline and a nice message announcing a sale. It had a nice photo of a sewing machine. What it did not have was a strong action device—a TRIGGER PHRASE—to prompt immediate action.

I told the gentleman to revise his ad and make his prospects sweat. "You have a nice sale that you're promoting, but you don't have a deadline," I told him. "Include a deadline in your next ad. Give the prospects a penalty for dragging their feet. Don't leave your offer open-ended, or they simply will not respond. Give an expiration date for the sale."

And if that doesn't work?" he said.

"Then limit your offer. Speak of the limited stock you have. Tell your prospects to HURRY! Then tell them if they don't act now, they may miss out on the great sale you're offering."

The businessman tried my suggestions and called me with a good report. "People are coming in asking if I have any machines left. I guess that ad is working," he said with a grin. "I guess you were right."

The above episode is no stranger to people in business, especially those who advertise. The truth is: Businesses everywhere spend money each day on pretty ads that don't work. And a basic reason many don't is they fail to use the trigger phrases, or as I like to call them, "secret persuaders." A good headline and bright colors may get your prospects' attention, but to get them to act—and respond to your offer—you need something more. You must give your prospects a legitimate reason—a strong inducement—for acting NOW.

This chapter is all about inducement. It's about using an incentive to induce immediate action. It focuses on the winning phrases—secret persuaders—that make people do what you want them to do about your offers.

What are Trigger Phrases?

Over the years, these prized phrases have been called different things. Robert Collier, in *The Robert Collier Letter Book*, called them "tested selling sentences," because the words have a proven track record of selling. In a broader sense, Herschell G. Lewis, author of *Direct Mail Copy that Sells*, describes the use of the phrases as "force communication." Why? Because the words compel prospects to act. In the book, *Direct Marketing Success*, Freeman F. Gosden, Jr. describes the phrases as an "action device" because they offer the reader a special benefit or offer for acting now.

At any rate, said Ted Nicholas, the words are emotional "magic words that make you rich." Others call the expressions "hooks" and "emotional incentives." But I prefer the word "trigger," because they ignite a certain feeling. They induce a certain action. They set off, like a trigger on a gun, a desired response. And when it comes to advertising, response is everything.

Trigger phrases can be used in any part of an ad, letter, brochure, or flier. Look at some of the ads in your local newspaper. Thumb through a magazine ... or review your direct-mail packages ... and you'll see trigger phrases used in headlines, body copy, subheads, and the close.

For this section, I will focus on the close—the call to action. "This is the spot where you win or lose the battle with inertia," writes Bob Stone in *Successful Direct Marketing Methods*. "Experienced advertisers know once a letter (or ad) is put aside or tossed into that file, they're out of luck. So wind up with a call for action and logical reason for acting now."

There are at least four types of trigger phrases you can use. Each, like a good headline and strong body copy, appeals to the four basic areas of human nature: greed, exclusivity, guilt, and fear.

Why Trigger Phrases Are So Important to Your Advertising

In a moment I will expound on the four types of trigger phrases, but for now let's consider the case for their use. Not surprisingly, their use is needed for several reasons.

Without a good reason, most people will not respond to an ad.

First, people are naturally *lazy*. They don't want to work or sweat for a good thing. They prefer entertainment or an event that doesn't require much effort. Without a good reason, most people will not respond to an ad.

Second, people are easily *distracted*. They are busy and tired. Many work long hours and have two or three jobs. They have families, numerous commitments, and a host of other things they'd rather do than answer your ad.

Third, people have other products or services that may be similar to yours. Thus, as an advertiser, you compete for their attention. You compete with the oceans of information that we see each day in the form of books, magazines, newsletters, Ezines, web pages, TV, radio, etc.

Fourth, people are *procrastinators*. They need the extra push to do not only what you want them to do, but even what they need to do. Initiative, in other words, is a strange bedfellow to man. "People are naturally dilatory," said Claude C. Hopkins. "They postpone, and a postponed action is too often forgotten."

In addition to those four factors, people also have limited amounts of money. They doubt you and they often hope for miracles. "Real people do not hold onto marketing materials for vast amounts of time waiting for the moment they need them," said Jeffrey Lant. "Most are tossed out the very day they're received. So why do you suppose that yours will be treated any differently?"

The Two Enemies of Response

Perhaps Maxwell Sackheim said it best when he wrote that every man, woman, and child has always been equipped with two enemies of advertising provided by nature, developed by individual circumstances—and encouraged by individual advertisers. Those two enemies are "indifference" and "inertia."

"Indifference is the number one gadget we have to overcome," Sackheim said. "Inertia is the law of physics which decrees that a body in motion or at rest resists change. People hate to bother changing their minds, their habits, their routines …. It takes tons of persuasion to make people do even the things they want to do."

So what's an advertiser to do? Unleash the power of the secret persuaders—the trigger phrases that induce immediate action. Let's take a look.

1. Trigger greed

A trigger phrase that appeals to the greed in us is a powerful tool for getting an immediate response. Since the beginning of time greed has been a strong motivator of human nature. And its power is seen in many pictures, like the old carrot that keeps the horse running. It's the cheese that catches the mice. It's the money that moves nations, and the rewards that help to guide children and adults. The truth is: We all want something of worth. We all desire to prosper. We want to grow and excel in one or more ventures. We all have a tendency to be greedy in one way or another.

A trigger phrase that appeals to the greed in us is a powerful tool for getting an immediate response.

To effectively use the greed trigger, you must show how the prospects can save, gain, or accomplish something by acting now. You have to show how their immediate action can enhance their status, increase their profits, beef up their savings, or whatever it is they desire.

When you pull the greed trigger, you say, "If you act NOW, you get THIS…!" You simply take the thing they want and dangle it before their face. You make their mouth water. You ignite their imagination and set their dreams on fire.

As I write this, I'm looking at a letter selling a marketing resource. Note how the writer pulled the greed trigger: "Return the enclosed $60 voucher when you order The Lifestyle Market Analyst and pay only $235. Act Now!"

The writer of the ad is saying: "You will get MORE! But you must act NOW to get it!" Don't we all want more? Don't we want it for little or nothing? Consider these examples:

- ▶ "Act now and you'll be guaranteed..."
- ▶ "If you order TODAY, you'll be able to..."
- ▶ "If you respond by _____, you'll get a FREE..."
- ▶ "Order now and pay later."
- ▶ "Send no money now."
- ▶ "Call now and SAVE ..."

The copywriter for *New Man* magazine used the greed trigger with the magical words, "FREE" and "Hurry."

> "Remember, your FREE ISSUE of NEW MAN magazine and FREE GIFT of John Trent's *Eight Steps to Intimacy* are yours to keep forever, even if you say 'no' to becoming a Charter Subscriber. Act now! Hurry!"

Here's an example from a letter selling *Writer's Digest*:

> "If you enclose payment now, two *extra* free issues will be added to your subscription, *and* your free copy of *Getting Published* will be shipped immediately."

As you can see, all of the above greed triggers imply gain ... savings ... improvement, etc. They shout, GET THIS! GET THAT! BUT YOU MUST ACT NOW!

2. Trigger feelings of exclusivity

Just as we all want to gain something of worth, we also want to *feel* like something of worth. We crave importance. And usually, that means being part of something with value. That may include a school, a special society, powerful political groups, a club, etc.

A hint of exclusivity can be triggered by using the word "invitation."

A hint of exclusivity can be triggered by using the word "invitation." Consider these two phrases from North Light Book Club:

> "This special trial membership is for artists who want to keep learning and growing...."
>
> "Just use the enclosed Invitation card to let us know which book you'd like FREE...."

In essence, when you pull the exclusive trigger, you tell the reader: "Remember, if you act now, you'll be joining the elite!" In a sense, you flatter the reader. You kiss up to the reader by making him or her feel important. You will note that the exclusivity trigger demonstrates that flattery really can get you anywhere, especially in marketing.

Here are some good examples:

- "Order now and be part of the few …"
- "Call now and become the envy of your friends …"
- "After we receive your order, we will send you a beautiful certificate suitable for framing."
- "Just think what your neighbors will say when they see you driving this …"

How do you like this one by American Express?

> "Quite frankly, the American Express Card is not for everyone. And not everyone who applies for card membership is approved."

Ted Nicholas made good use of the exclusivity trigger to sell his seminars.

> "96 participants total is all I'll accept…. Since I will be working closely with you, I reserve the right to decline any seminar applicant for any reason."

Did you see how Nicholas also used the fear trigger by suggesting the reader will miss out if he or she doesn't act now? That's good copy.

3. Trigger guilt

Guilt is defined as a feeling of responsibility for wrongdoing. Pull the guilt trigger to make your prospects feel bad about failing to take action. You pull this trigger and say: "Miss this chance, and you may never forgive yourself."

Although guilt triggers are used most often in fundraising copy, they can still be effectively used in business copy. In direct mail, you see the triggers used in lift letters:

"I don't understand …" or, "Have I misled you?"

The phrases are almost apologetic. They break down hard sales talk by making you *feel* for the seller. Consider this one to a former magazine subscriber:

> "It hurts to lose an old friend."

Here are a few more examples:

- "So please act today. The plants and animals living on our preserves need your support to survive."—**The Nature Conservancy**
- "But we must act <u>NOW</u> while this window of opportunity is still open. Who knows how long this door will stay open for us?"—**Nora Lam Ministries**

Pull the guilt trigger to make your prospects feel bad about failing to take action.

▶ I know I'm asking a lot. But isn't our nation's future and our children's future worth it? I will anxiously look for your completed referendum and gift of support to arrive in my mailbox in the next few days."— **Christian Coalition**

4. Trigger Fear

Although greed, exclusivity, and guilt are strong motivators for pulling response, fear may well be the most powerful. "Greed, Guilt and Exclusivity are all Herculean as selling arguments," said Herschell G. Lewis, "but Fear is the strongest, because it's the one motivator that can cause the reader to lose sleep."

Lewis's view was also articulated many years ago by Victor Schwab, author of *How to Write a Good Advertisement*. Schwab wrote:

> ... the appeal of 'fear of loss' can often far outweigh the appeal of 'the desire of gain.' I have known men who refused to risk any amount of money in gambling—simply because the only amount of money that would give them any considerable kick in winning would have had to be sizeable enough to distress them greatly if they were to lose it. That is why good copy often utilizes both arguments: what you may lose, risk, or waste if you do not buy the product; and what you may gain or save if you do buy it.

Your best trigger, then, is the fear trigger. It's about pain and loss. You pull it to tell prospects they will continue in pain unless they call you or accept your offer. Or you tell them what they may lose by delaying to act.

How is it used? Consider this example from *Sales & Marketing Management*: "If you reject our risk-free offer, look at a small sample of the upcoming articles you'll miss."

The point is clear: If you delay, you will be punished! But why is fear such a strong motivator? It's like the old saying: "I may not stay up all night to make a hundred dollars, but I'll sure stay up to keep from losing it. Charles Margolis of Speedibooks once gave a charming illustration on this point:

Lesson from a Fish

Did you ever fish for bluegills? You lower the bait when you still-fish. Sometimes when the water is clear, you can see the fish approach the bait, but they don't take it. Instead, they swim away a bit. You hold the bait still. The bluegill swims back. It nudges the bait, but doesn't take it. The fish swims away again. After a moment, he starts back, slowly. As he approaches the

*F*ear is the strongest, because it's the one motivator that can cause the reader to lose sleep.

bait, you slowly draw it away. The fish then follows. But you draw the bait away—again. The fish strikes and now you have him.

"What happened?" asked Margolis. "You threatened to take away the bait. He didn't want it all that much. But as soon as he was threatened with the loss, he decided he really did want it. So you won in the battle of wits."

That is precisely what happens when you pull the fear trigger. You threaten the prospects with loss. You make them hungry, then threaten to take away the food … the benefits … the dream … the opportunity. Yet, to make the trigger work, you must be sincere, specific, and believable. In other words, don't just say, "Prices will go up soon." Instead, say, "On August 1, prices will go up to $29.95."

Instead of saying, "Act now and we'll send you a free gift," say, "If you respond by Dec. 15, we will send you a FREE copy of *Writing Books Made Easy* to help you get published."

If your supply really is limited, then say it. But say it with sincerity—and in a credible manner. For example: "Only 112 copies are left. Our success has been greater than all our expectations. Once gone, they are gone forever."

Take a look at these examples:

- "Act today. I can only guarantee to accept your order if I receive it <u>within</u> <u>the</u> <u>next</u> <u>two</u> <u>weeks</u>." —**Alan Shawn Feinstein**

- "Since yearly demand for the FORTUNE Diary is great, we urge you to order a.s.a.p.—in time for the new year." —*Fortune*

- "You are preapproved for a Chase Visa with *NO ANNUAL FEE* and a low, variable APR for purchases that is now just 6.9%. But this is a special, *limited-time* offer, so I urge you to respond now—before it expires." —**Chase**

- Last chance to lock-in at current low rate! Price increase coming in February." —*Consumer Reports*

The Real Winner In Compelling Copy

By now you can see that trigger phrases are made up of strong emotional words—and not words that merely tickle the intellect. The reason is simple: When emotion and intellect compete for attention—and for action—emotion wins. That's especially true in selling. It's commonly agreed that people buy with their hearts and not with their heads. Only after they have made a purchase do they begin to justify their reasons for making it. That's why it's important for copy to sell the sizzle and not the steak.

"Does a quiet intellectual argument sell better than excitement? Usually not," says Herschell G. Lewis. "Replace intellectual words with emotional words and you'll sell more because you'll TRIGGER an emotional response."

Chapter 7

5 Tips for Making Your Prospects Hungry:
The Rules for Enticing Your Prospects, Clients, and Customers by Turning Your Sales Message into Mouth-Watering Prose

HAVE YOU READ ANYTHING RECENTLY BY ERNEST HEMINGWAY? IF not, then perhaps you should. I say this because his unique style of writing provides some good lessons for writing strong sales copy.

You see, Hemingway was not a copywriter (although he reportedly tried it at one time). Yet, when he wrote about food, he had a way of making you hungry. His "prose, shorn of the stylistically convoluted Victorian filigrees of nineteenth- and early-twentieth-century writing, evoked an intense appreciation of life's perils—and pleasures," wrote Neil A. Grauer in *Cigar Aficionado* (August 1999). "Few have ever equaled his skill at writing about war's horrors—or the wonders of food and drink."

He "actually makes you hungry and thirsty for the fare he describes," observed Kenneth S. Lynn in the biography, *Hemingway*. In the movie, "City of Angels," Nicolas Cage's character makes a similar observation about Hemingway.

Hemingway's penchant for creating desires and strong appetites in readers offers a lesson for anyone wanting to nab prospects or catch customers.

In a moment, I'm going to show you what can be gained from his style. But first, I want to show you an excerpt from his short story, "Big Two-hearted River: Part I":

> Nick put the frying pan on the grill over the flames. He was hungrier. The beans and spaghetti warmed. Nick stirred them and mixed them together. They began to bubble, making little bubbles that rose with difficulty to the surface. There was a good smell. Nick got out a bottle of tomato catchup and cut four slices of bread. The little bubbles were coming faster now. Nick sat down beside the fire and lifted the frying pan off. He poured about half the contents out into the tin plate. It spread slowly on the plate.

Can you see the picture here? Can't you almost taste the beans and spaghetti? Does it make you hungry? Making people "hungry" is the job of any piece of sales literature. Whether you're selling cars or snow cones, real estate or health care, the aim is to entice your prospects and lure them in for the sale. To do that, you need mouth-watering words that excite; words that tickle and tease. You need words that create an insatiable hunger for the product or service you're offering.

Here are some ways you can make that happen.

1. Paint a picture

It's been said that one picture is worth a thousand words. Yet, says one writer, a few well-chosen words are worth a thousand pictures!

If you have a good photo of your product, use it. Good pictures are always useful. But without a photo, you must rely on words—colorful words—to paint the picture you need. It's been said that one picture is worth a thousand words. Yet, says one writer, a few well-chosen words are worth a thousand pictures! I agree.

When writing sales copy, you can paint a vivid picture by using words that appeal to two or more of the five senses. An example of this was found recently on a box of popcorn:

> "When you want popcorn, you gotta have Butter-Licious. When you dream of munching that fluffy, buttery-rich snack … long for that irresistible aroma … crave that luscious, savory butter sensation … it's gotta be JOLLY TIME Butter-Licious Microwave Popcorn!"

2. Use precise details

Hemingway had an eye for details. Using a terse, lean, and understated style, he told his stories with detailed descriptions. Because of the specific and precise manner in which he wrote, readers could identify with his characters.

They felt what the characters felt. The same is true in advertising. Copy laced with specifics is much more believable than bland copy filled with generalities.

Ross von Hoelscher observed that years ago, you could write a headline that simply stated, "New book shows you how to make big money!"

"Those days are gone," he said. "Today's potential responder wants specifics, and is more than a little skeptical."

A good example of an ad using specific copy is being used by Laurie Kaye to sell a real estate program. Her headline reads: "How I made $382,733 in 1997." Now, if you're in real estate, you'll find this ad to be irresistible.

3. Use repetition

Although Hemingway is known for his mastery of the simple and strong declarative sentence, he also made full use of repetition to engage readers. In the aforementioned short story, he told us several times that Nick Adams was hungry.

Repetition in an academic paper may be frowned upon. But in an ad or direct-mail package, repetition is magic. Generally, prospects are lazy and reluctant in responding to sales messages. To get their attention, you must hit them over the head several times with your offer. The more you stress your key points, the more likely your prospects will remember them and respond.

Repetition in an academic paper may be frowned upon. But in an ad or direct-mail package, repetition is magic.

In a TV commercial, your key point may be mentioned at the top and bottom of your script. Follow the same procedure in your sales letter. If you're using a full direct-mail package, your offer may be highlighted in the letter, brochure, lift note, and response card.

As I write this, I'm looking at a direct-mail package from *Writer's Digest*. A teaser on the front of the outside envelope screams:

"We're giving away $25,000.00 Blockbuster Writing Grant."

This message is repeated on the back of the envelope. It is mentioned throughout a four-page letter. It is noted on a colorful brochure as well as on the response card. In this package, repetition is king—and quite effective.

4. Show reactions

Benefits are the end result of what people get when they use your product or service. Will they be richer? Then stress that in your writing. Will they gain friends and influence people? Stress that. Whatever you can picture them doing as a result of your offer, use that to whet their appetites.

When Hemingway wrote about people eating, he often showed their reaction. If they enjoyed a slice of ham, he showed it. And that, I remind you, is what we must do with sales copy. When people react positively to our products or services, we must show that in our sales message. Their enjoyment is one of the benefits that is worth stressing.

Here's what Hemingway wrote about Nick Adams:

> He was very hungry.... He took a full spoonful from the plate (of beans and spaghetti). "Chrise," Nick said, "Geezus Chrise," he said happily. He ate the whole plateful before he remembered the bread. Nick finished the second plateful with the bread, mopping the plate shiny.

When you show people enjoying a good meal—or using a good product—you create desire in the people you're trying to reach. *You make them hungry!*

5. Tell a story

If you want to invigorate your sales literature, then use a story as the greater portion of your sales message or as an anecdote

People everywhere love stories. They remember them and they share them. If you want to invigorate your sales literature, then use a story as the greater portion of your sales message or as an anecdote—a mini-story within your message. One of the most successful ads of all time was written as a story. It began with the famous words, "They laughed when I sat down at the piano, but when I started to play ..." John Caples, who wrote the ad, used a compelling narrative to sell a home-study course for the U.S. School of Music.

Stories in the form of anecdotes are equally useful. "Anecdotes are great reader pleasers," wrote Gary Provost in *100 Ways to Improve Your Writing*. "They are written like fiction, often contain dialogue, and reduce a large issue to a comprehensible size by making it personal."

Provost went on to say that writing a short, colorful anecdote is "one of the most compelling ways to begin an article, query letter, or business proposal."

The five points I offer here have a proven track record. Try them and see if they don't work for you. Think of Hemingway and make your prospects hungry!

Chapter 8

10 Tips for Unleashing the Power of Classified Ads:
Everything You Need to Know to Create Winners

AN EAGER REAL ESTATE AGENT WANTED TO USE CLASSIFIEDS TO GEN-
erate leads for a home she had to sell. But to her surprise, her boss looked at her with a cold stare and said, "Honey, the people we want don't read classifieds."
Unfortunately, there are a number of myths associated with classifieds. And not surprisingly these views are often held by people who have lost money on classifieds or they simply have not done their homework. The scenario, in a sense, is like the classic story about the fox and the grapes. When the fox failed to get the grapes, he dismissed them as being no good anyway.

One of the mistaken ideas about classifieds is that people don't read them. According to this claim, people don't read classifieds because of their small print and the fact that they're cluttered among too many other ads. However, the fact is people *do* read these ads. The proof is in the fact that the classified sections of magazines and newspapers are essential elements of those publications. Not a few of the ads are repeated daily or month after month. No one in their right mind would continue to run ads if they did not show a profit.

Another mistaken view is that classifieds are only read by people in the low-income bracket. This view suggests that classifieds are beneath the interests of high-level clients. People with money are more impressed by large display ads. Hence the reason for companies purchasing full-page image ads. Again, the fact is that classifieds are read—and used—by people of all backgrounds.

Although some may read them religiously, looking for bargains and unusual offers, others read them in search of solutions, or to find good business opportunities, among other things.

Then there's the view that classifieds are ineffective. This view will likely be shared by a copywriter or ad agency who wants to design a bigger ad for your business and charge you higher rates. However, the claim flies in the face of research that shows that profits can indeed be found in the little ads. Sometimes this view is held by someone who focuses on all the ads that did not work; they do not take into account the mistakes or variables that may have led to the failure. It's a given that classifieds will not work for all products and services. The reason is that some of the offers require more space and more copy to explain. But all things being equal, for every classified that loses money, there's another one that is making money. Therefore it is not always good to focus on the negative.

All things being equal, for every classified that loses money, there's another one that is making money.

No one can deny the value of formal research on this issue, but such research is not necessary. As suggested before, just take a look at the ads in your favorite publications and make note of the ones that are repeated.

As you review this section—and contemplate the use of small ads—keep in mind that bigger is not always better. In his book, *The 33 Ruthless Rules of Local Advertising*, Michael Corbett cited a study, the Daniel Starch Report, about the size and readership of newspaper ads. In terms of retail advertising, the study noted:

▶ A full-page ad will provide a very small percentage of increased reading, seeing, associating, or noting of your ad, versus a half page ad, but you pay twice as much with most papers.

▶ A half-page ad will provide only a slightly larger percentage of increased seeing, reading, associating, or noting of your ad versus a quarter-page ad, but you pay twice as much with most papers.

These results are not surprising, as David Ogilvy once mentioned similar results regarding full-page ads in magazines.

A Few Advantages of Using Classifieds

Although people can be mistaken about the value of classifieds, this is not to suggest that classifieds are without limitations. The truth is, because of the size of the ad, it does carry a number of built-in limitations, so to speak. For instance: It does not allow for photos; it is not suitable for detailed copy; it is surrounded by a mass of other ads; it doesn't provide space for demonstrating the benefits of a product; it doesn't allow space for testimonials, etc.

While all of these issues may rightly be a concern, it is useful to remember that classifieds have advantages that should not be ignored.

- ▶ **Classifieds are inexpensive.** This is perhaps the biggest advantage of using this form of advertising. Payment is generally based on the number of words or the lines of copy used in the ad. Given the low cost, you can actually run an entire series of classifieds for the price of one full-page ad. The inexpensive nature of the ad means you can reach out to your prospects on a regular basis without breaking your bank account.

- ▶ **Classifieds are great for low-cost testing.** If you wanted to test various elements of a large display ad, it would indeed be costly. The reason is obvious: Each time you test, you'd have to pay for the space of the whole ad. On the other hand, classifieds allow you to inexpensively test copy throughout a series—and at the cost of a single large display ad.

- ▶ **Classifieds are ideal for testing new concepts.** Whenever copywriter Ted Nicholas was brainstorming for a new book title, he used to narrow his list of ideas down to a few titles. Then he would run classifieds and use the titles as headlines for each ad. The ad that pulled the biggest response would provide him with the winning title for his new book.

Obviously, this process can be easily applied to other products and services. In fact, I'd go so far as to say it should be a mandatory requirement not only for measuring the effectiveness of your classified, but for any marketing campaign.

- ▶ **Classifieds are well-read.** Do people really read these tiny ads in the back of newspapers and magazines? Most assuredly. "There's a unique fascination with classified ads," noted Melvin Powers, author of *How to Get Rich in Mailorder*. "People read them even when they aren't looking for anything in particular."

While thumbing through an issue of *The Record Herald* (Waynesboro, PA), I spotted a small display ad in the back section of the paper. It used the headline: "When you plant a classified ad, you get a big crop of replies!" This may seem corny, but it's true, nonetheless. Especially when you have all the right elements in place.

- ▶ **Classifieds require less copy.** Ok. So this is a no-brainer. Brevity is an

Classifieds allow you to inexpensively test copy throughout a series—and at the cost of a single large display ad.

obvious feature of these small ads. Whereas a cold call by phone or in person can be costly to a small business, a good classified can generate leads on a continual basis—and save you time—on a small budget.

▶ **Classifieds are great for generating leads.** The two-step approach means that you make an offer in your ad that prompts the reader to make contact with you. You invite them to contact you by phone, mail, or e-mail, etc. When the contact is made, you simply follow-up with a sales call or direct-mail package.

Ideally, you would generate leads by offering something FREE! This could be a booklet, newsletter, more information, 30-minute consultation, discount, CD brochure, or catalog.

Another benefit with this approach is that it allows you to build a mailing list of prospects and customers. Once you have their contact information, you can stay in touch with them by publishing a newsletter.

▶ **Classifieds can be used for local, regional, and national audiences.** It's been said that the classified is the one tool that allows the little guy (or gal) to be more competitive. It enables the small businessperson to reach his or her audience on a small budget, no matter where they live. Because of the low cost of the ads, one can actually start a business from home or simply promote an existing business to a larger audience.

Attempting a national ad campaign with full-page ads is simply out of the question for many small businesses. Yet, such a campaign, though smaller, is certainly doable when classifieds are used. Of course, this all depends on the products and services being offered.

Some of the most common mistakes in classified advertising are:

▶ **The ad has a bland headline that is too general.** A good headline is strong and specific. It calls out to your audience. It sounds off with a benefit or it alerts your audience to a problem. Both your headline and body copy should be written with a sense of urgency. Readers must feel a need to "LOOK HERE!" at your ad, and "ACT NOW!" to receive what you promise.

▶ **The ad is vague or misleading.** Sometimes one word can make the difference in an otherwise good classified. Take this example:

Many years ago I promoted a book entitled, "Big Bucks from Little Sketches." I wrote a classified and used the headline, "BIG BUCKS FOR LITTLE SKETCHES." To my surprise, most of the people who responded inquired about me paying them for their artwork. They thought I was looking to hire artists. Well, I examined the ad and changed the word "for" to "from" and ran another test. This time the ad read, "BIG BUCKS FROM LITTLE SKETCHES." To my delight, the readers responded with questions about how to make money with their sketches. Bingo!

The lesson here is obvious: If you give a prospect a chance to misunderstand your ad, chances are, they will. So make sure your ad says exactly what you want it to say. Nothing less. Nothing more. Weed out all vague expressions. Be specific and precise.

▶ **The ad attempts to sell directly.** Although selling directly is possible, it is unlikely to make a profit. If you're selling a $5 item, you might generate a few orders, but it would take much more than a few to make it worth your while.

Classifieds are best used for generating leads. This is especially important when you have a high-end product or service you want to sell.

Remember, classifieds are simply too small to allow for a strong sales message. They are best for catching attention, teasing, and piquing the interest of your prospects.

▶ **The ad is too wordy.** The most effective classifieds are written in telegraphic style (think of the old telegraph messages). They use short, snappy phrases and abbreviations. Everything is cut to bare minimum, but without being cryptic. Of course, the key benefit of this approach is that it saves you money. You may well be an excellent writer, but the classified section is not the place to showcase your literary talent.

▶ **The ad is featured under the wrong category.** Classified sections have many categories. Everything from "Books" and "Education" to "Garage sales" and "Business opportunities." You may have a great offer, but if it appears under the wrong categories, your advertising efforts will be in vain. Keep in mind that people who read classifieds often focus on the categories that interest them. Determine what your audience needs and where they go for answers. Then place your ad under the category where your audience is most likely to see it.

▶ **The ad is used to sell only one product.** Mail order experts discovered long ago that classifieds are best used for selling multiple products. Generally, the first product is one that's inexpensive and is offered through the ad. When readers respond to receive this product (also called a "loss leader"), they receive the product along with a catalog of other related products.

The most effective classifieds are written in telegraphic style.

Simply put: The cost of advertising makes it highly unlikely to make a profit with a single product.

A business needs repeat business in order to prosper. To generate repeat business, you need a product or service that you can sell to customers on an ongoing basis. Your business must become the preferred source, or even the "one-stop shop," for the products or services they seek.

So before you run your classifieds, make sure you have a list of follow-up products or services that will keep them coming back for more.

How to Write a Winner

Now that you understand the uses of classifieds and you have your products ready to go, it is time to begin working on your own winning copy. Following is a list of suggestions for creating a classified that gets results.

1. Select the right publications

As a small businessperson, you will save money and avoid waste when you choose the best publications for your classified ad campaign.

This has been suggested elsewhere but it bears repeating. As a small businessperson, you will save money and avoid waste when you choose the best publications for your classified ad campaign. What are the best publications?

First, they are the newspapers and magazines that are read by your audience. Second, they are the same ones that are used by your competitors. Third, they are the publications that have a strong classified section. Typically, magazines with a large classified section are effective in pulling orders.

Although magazines and newspapers will undoubtedly be at the top of your list, do not rule out other publications. Consider newsletters published by the local Chamber of Commerce or perhaps an e-zine that targets your audience. "You must familiarize yourself with all the publications that reach the people who can buy from you," noted Dr. Jeffrey Lant in *No More Cold Calls.*

2. Request a media kit

A media kit is nothing more than a folder of information that provides detailed advertising data about a particular publication. In addition to the cost of the ads (also called "ad rate card"), the kit provides you with circulation figures, deadlines, and information on the demographics served by the publications.

Media kits are free for the asking and they usually come with a sample copy of the publication.

3. Examine the classified section

Once you have a few of the publications read by your audience, take a close look at the classified section. How large is it? What's the cost? Who are your competitors? What are the available categories under which your ad might appear? Must you pay by word or by line?

Examine the graphics. Are bold headlines allowed? What about headlines in all caps? Is color allowed? Borders or boxes around the copy?

If you study several issues of a magazine, you will find that certain ads are repeated over and over. This is a sure sign of a winning ad.

4. Select the appropriate category

Take a look at the category used by your competitor. Is it the best one for your product or service? The fact that classifieds have categories is a plus for this type of advertising, according to Jay Conrad Levinson, author of *Guerrilla Advertising*. "[Classifieds] are more powerful than ever, because there are more classifications than ever, letting you pinpoint prospects," he wrote.

5. Write a powerful headline

Since the headline is the most important part of any ad, you would be wise to spend as much time as possible in brainstorming until you come up with a winner. Begin with a list of all the benefits of your product or service. Select the one that is most likely to grab your prospects.

Then write a headline that incorporates this major benefit.

If you struggle with using a benefit in your headline, consider a headline that focuses on the problem or need of your prospects. As with the benefits, simply make a list of all the problems that your product or service solves. Then pick the one most likely to grab the attention of your prospects. Once this is done, write a provocative headline that calls attention to the problem.

Since shorter is usually better with classifieds, try to write a headline with six words or less. Sometimes, when stressing a problem, you can get away with one or two words as a headline. Example: "BAD BREATH!" Or you could write something like, "YELLOW TEETH!"

In addition to using benefits and problems in your copy, you might also consider calling out to your audience. "MEN WITH BAD BACKS!" Or you may write, "EMPLOYERS WITH HIGH TURNOVERS!"

"If you can find a one-word headline that will attract the right prospects, such as 'Accounting,' 'Deaf,' or 'Loans,' it will probably be your best head-

Since shorter is usually better with classifieds, try to write a headline with six words or less.

line," according to John Caples. "The reason is because it can be set in big type without taking up much room."

Note: Classified headlines can be more effective when they printed in bold type or they are written in all caps.

6. Write a complete sales message about your product or service

One of the best ways to create a winning classified is to first write a lengthy sales message about your product or service and then cut it down to size.

One of the best ways to create a winning classified is to first write a lengthy sales message about your product or service and then cut it down to size. Here's how to start:

First, make a list of all the essential elements. This list should include headline, benefits, offer, call to action, contact information (mail, phone, e-mail, or web site) and some type of code that allows you to know where prospects saw your ad.

Second, while using your ultimate benefit, write a detailed paragraph that shows how your product or service will help your prospects. Will it save them money? Improve their health? Ensure a job promotion?

7. Determine the required length and begin cutting

How many words can you afford in your ad? Will you test an ad with 30 words or 20? Three lines of copy or four? Once you know this, it is time to start cutting.

Simply go through the copy and cut all unnecessary words. Eliminate sentences that don't add to the message. Remove introductions and leave only those words with the strongest selling power.

8. Use telegraphic language

Write "as if you were sending a cablegram (in the old days) and you had to pay fifty cents a word," advised John Caples. This is good advice when you consider that readers of classifieds are accustomed to this type of language. They've come to expect it and can usually read it without a problem.

Therefore, instead of writing, "I will send you a free report," write: "Free report!" Instead of, "You can use this widget to save money," simply write, "Save cash!" Instead of using, "This widget is fast and easy to use," you could write, "Easy! Fast!" Instead of writing, "Guaranteed results or your money back," write: "Guaranteed!"

9. Abbreviate where necessary

Certain abbreviations are easily understood by respective audiences. If you specialize in Business-to-Business services, then your audience will certainly understand the use of "B2B" in your ad. Most readers would understand "Bklt" to mean "Booklet."

Since you will be paying by the word (or lines of copy), you want to tell your story in as few words as possible. This idea is particularly useful when writing your contact information. Example: Instead of "Post Office Box 10," write: "Bx 10."

Note: *Don't forget to code every ad, as this will allow you to track results. Some businesses use different names to call in each ad: "Call Mary" will appear in one ad; "Call John" will appear in another one. Sometimes this is done to test publications: "Call Mary" will appear in magazine A; and "Call John" will appear in magazine B.*

Another method of coding is to include a suite number in your address: "Suite A" will appear in one ad or one publication, while "Suite B" will appear in another.

10. Write a second classified and begin testing

Write a second headline and test it in the same publication. Measure the results. Or, keep the same headline and change the offer. Run this in the same publication and then measure the results.

Once you've determined which ad pulled the most response, begin testing it in different publications.

Chapter 9

10 Pointers for Crafting a Great Advertorial:

What Every Advertiser Should Know about Editorial-Type Ads

THERE COMES A TIME WHEN ALL SMALL BUSINESSES MUST PAY FOR their publicity. They've exhausted their use of the press release. They've used up all of their feature story ideas. They've depleted their finances for direct-mail packages. Now they're left with one final marketing tool to generate hot leads and push their profits to the next level. It's advertising.

When you reach that point, it's not the time to think fancy. It's time to think response. Instead of the typical ads that you see in most publications—newspapers and magazines—think *advertorial*—the kind of ad that actually looks like a real news story or other editorial matter.

Advertorials generally have a good track record. They are to print what Infomercials are to TV. They may be corny to the uninformed but, like the TV Infomercials, they work just the same.

A Tip from *Reader's Digest*

In his classic advertising primer *Tested Advertising Methods*, John Caples right-fully noted that editorial-style ads get high reading. As an example, he referred to a test conducted by *Reader's Digest*, in which an ad for Adolph's Salt Substitute was designed to look like a magazine article. Here's what he said:

> A split-run test of two mail order ads showed that an ad that looked like a magazine article pulled 81 percent more orders than the identical copy, set in ad-style.

Incredible, isn't it?

Copywriter Joe Vitale observed that "readers are up to 500 times more likely to read an advertorial than a straight ad." Results like that would compel me to at least try the advertorial.

Although much has been said about advertising in print media, it goes without saying that most of the concepts provided here will also apply to the Internet.

For instance, veteran copywriter Clayton Makepeace has been extremely successful in writing advertorials for the Internet. In an interview published in his newsletter, *The Total Package* (May 23, 2006), he surmised that effectiveness on the web was because people are used to receiving free information on the web. He explained:

> If you begin a promotion that says, 'Hey, here's my product. Isn't it beautiful?' You're really saying, 'Hey, you know, if you read this I'm gonna try to sell you something.' Whereas, on the other hand, if you go in with an advertorial appeal and you talk to the person about fulfilling their desires or assuaging their fears or eliminating their frustration, by the time you get around to the sales copy, you're their friend and advocate instead of a salesman trying to get them to sign the dotted line.

A Good Example

When was the last time you saw a good advertorial—written for a small business? In my own case, I see few on the local level but dozens on the national level that appear primarily in business opportunity magazines.

However, there was one I saw a while back that caught my eye. It was for a nonprofit organization, Food For The Poor of Deerfield Beach, Fla. The advertorial appeared as a full-page ad in *Christianity Today* (December 2000). While I don't know the results of its response, I'm willing to bet that it was a good one.

You see, the ad looks and feel like the other articles appearing in that magazine. It has two strong headlines, a byline, three photos, and a NO logo. And that's the secret.

Would you like to try your hand at developing a good advertorial? Then remember these factors:

1. Study the publication in which your ad will appear

Get a sense of its style. Check out the competition—the kind of ads they use. Look at the typeface and size of the type. Study the headlines and graphics. Then, as much as possible, try to model your ad after those articles.

2. Inquire about the policy on advertorials

Some publications frown on ads that look like their editorial copy. As a result, they insist that ads have some noticeable differences. OK. That's understood. If you must use a different typeface or font, so be it. But you can still make your piece look like an article.

As a rule, most publications will require the word "advertisement" printed in small letters at the top or bottom of your ad. Some will only use such ads in special sections.

3. Determine an appropriate size

To look like an article, your advertorial must be of a size that's similar to the actual editorial copy.

To look like an article, your advertorial must be of a size that's similar to the actual editorial copy. Ideally, you'd want it to be a full or half-page in magazines. In newspapers, consider nothing smaller than a quarter page (unless, of course, you can only afford something smaller).

4. Write a suitable headline

Unlike the headlines in your brochures and direct-mail pieces, a suitable advertorial headline is one that is newsy or very similar to those in the publication in which it appears. In the typical newspaper, you won't see a headline loaded with fluff or superlatives that brag about an organization. Instead, you see headlines that are simple and straightforward. Food For The Poor used: "Poor Families Rely On Trash For Food Clothing—Survival."

At the bottom, another headline appears: "Food For The Poor's Outreach Creates Hope Among Riverton's 'Dump Dwellers.'" You might consider borrowing headlines from your press releases.

5. Use a byline

That gives it credibility, particularly if the name is recognized by readers. Pen names also are useful. Even if it's not well-known, the appearance of a byline will suggest that the piece was "authored." Food For The Poor uses "Special Report by Geraldine Hemmings."

6. Use photos with captions

Captions do not appear in the Food For The Poor's ad. But typically, an advertorial is stronger when its photos have some kind of caption written underneath, like those you see in newspapers. As with the "article," include a byline for the photographer.

7. Open and close with a bang

As with all forms of good communication, your lead paragraph should hook the reader—just like the articles in the publication you've chosen. Don't forget to close with something that moves the reader to action.

8. Sprinkle with quotes

Enliven your piece with quotes from real people, real experts. Use the quotes as testimonials or to back up certain claims. Insert them throughout your copy. Use them the way a typical journalist would.

9. Break up copy with subheads

Depending on the length of your copy, subheads can make the material more reader-friendly. Use them to draw attention to crucial parts in your ad.

10. Include the "call to action" and contact information

Your piece may look like an article, but it still is an ad. For that reason, don't slack in calling the prospect to action. Create a sense of urgency and tell them exactly what you want them to do—and when!

You may or may not use a coupon (and you probably shouldn't), but if you do, include contact information on both the coupon and in the copy of the ad. That way, if the coupon is torn out and another person reads the publication, he or she may still have access to your organization.

With these ideas in mind, you should be able to create a winning advertorial. Examine your budget and see if you can't test an idea. Start small—with small publications or small ads—and work your way up.

Your piece may look like an article, but it still is an ad. For that reason, don't slack in calling the prospect to action.

Are advertorials effective in every case? Hardly. But neither are other copywriting tools. Even so, I still suggest that if you have the budget, the advertorial is worth a good test. After you've tried it, send me a note. Let me know how it turns out.

Chapter 10

5 Essential Elements of a Winning Direct-Mail Package:
The Tried and True Ingredients for Improving Your Direct-Mail Campaign

A FRIEND ONCE SAID THAT HE HATES JUNK MAIL AND THAT HE TOSSES it into the trash as soon as he gets it. However, a few days later I saw this friend at a video store. He was about to pay for his DVDs when he handed the cashier a coupon. It was a coupon he had received in the mail. So the lesson is clear: People may despise advertising in the mail, but when they see something they like, they respond just like all other customers. Hence, the beauty of marketing through the mail.

However, when it comes to using direct mail, you may have to change your thinking: Despite all the claims being made about the power of the Internet and e-commerce, direct mail is still alive and well. Today it is sometimes referred to as "snail mail" and more often, "junk mail," but it remains an essential tool for direct-response marketing campaigns.

In an article titled, "The Current State of Snail Mail" (*Target Marketing*, January 2003), veteran copywriter Denny Hatch made an interesting comment about direct mail: "With the Can Spam Act and do-not-call laws, snail mail is once again the workhorse of direct marketing," he wrote. "And all direct marketers better learn how to write it, design it and find precisely the right people to send it to, or they will wind up in the same career ash heap as the smarty-pants wizards of the later 1990s."

That suggests that direct mail is not only viable, but also critical to effective marketing. It is ideal for any product or service. Besides allowing you to reach prospects by name and according to specific demographics, it also allows you to effectively test what works and what doesn't work.

Given the importance of direct mail as a powerful marketing tool, it would be useful to take a look at the key elements that make up a complete direct-mail package. Some of these elements are more important than others, but a review of each of them will give you a sense of how direct mail works. Simply put, direct mail, in the traditional sense, consists of an envelope (with or without a teaser), a letter (any length), a brochure, order form, lift note, and a business reply envelope. In addition to these elements, you also need a mailing list. However, this section will focus on the direct-mail package and not list management or the selection of lists.

Let's take a closer look.

1. The Envelope

What's inside your envelope may be the key to a big sale, but unless it is opened, the sale will never happen.

What's inside your envelope may be the key to a big sale, but unless it is opened, the sale will never happen. For this reason, the envelope plays a critical role in direct-mail. Although some marketers have found success using blank envelopes, many believe every direct-mail package should include a teaser that will move the prospect to open the envelope.

The fundamental nature and purpose of a good teaser is to grab attention and pique one's curiosity. It should offer only enough information that will move a person to action. A good way to learn to write teasers is by watching the television news. Consider this scenario:

It's around 8 p.m. You're in the comfort of your living room and watching your favorite TV show when a reporter pops up during a commercial break. You'd planned to be in bed around 10, but the reporter says something that grabs your attention: "A local businessman has been arrested for raping a 12-year-old girl. Join us at 11 and find out what police discovered when they followed him home."

You squint and frown, wondering who that could be. "How could that happen in my neighborhood?" you wonder.

A few minutes later, the same "news brief" appears, telling you to stay tuned and to join the news program at 11.

What will you do?

Chances are, you'll stay up for that program. Why? Because curiosity got the best of you. The reporter said something that got your attention. And it was something that piqued your curiosity, compelling you to stay up later and watch the 11 o'clock news program.

When a TV reporter says, "Join us tonight" or "Tune in tonight, and find out …" she is expressing the aim of every direct mail package, which says, "Open me *now*!" With that view in mind, consider using teasers that:

Offer news

As you would expect, news is the bread and butter of good TV journalism. Reporters thrive on fast-breaking stories. They live for reports that affect the people they serve. Some will sell their soul for a major exposé. For those reasons, you might see a teaser that promises hot or late-breaking stories.

Example: "A new report shows the city's drinking water might be contaminated. Join us tonight and find out how!"

In addition to providing hot news, that teaser addresses a problem and it connects it to the viewers. The same should be done with the copy on your envelopes. Simply capture something that will be new (or even shocking) to your prospects. But instead of spelling it out on the envelope, leave them hanging. You won't say, "Join us tonight," like the TV reporters. But you could say, "Look inside." or "Details inside!"

Warn of problems

Reporters like to be first in reporting hot stories. They also want to be the first to alert you of approaching danger or upcoming disasters.

Example: "Three hundred factory workers will lose their jobs tomorrow. We'll tell you why and where … when you join us at 11."

Again, there's news in that teaser. But at the same time, it strikes a nerve. If you're a factory worker and you see that teaser, you will tune in for the details. As with any legitimate news item, the TV teaser is relevant. It hits close to home. And that is the job of a teaser in print, particularly where fear is a motivating factor.

Prospects must be made to feel that they too could be affected by the approaching danger. The teaser on the outer envelope should make them feel that they too might be victims of some crisis.

Prospects must be made to feel that they too could be affected by the approaching danger

Focus on issues

Local reporters are notorious for localizing national issues. Another word for that is "piggybacking." They take a hot issue that's being discussed nationally, put a spin on it, and then tailor it to a local audience.

When the Columbine school shooting made national news, local stations everywhere began riding the issues, offering all kinds of teasers about violence in the local schools.

Example: *"Are your children safe in school? Are they playing with guns behind your back? Find out at 11!"*

Now think about your business. Can you tie it in with a hot-button issue? If so, then write a teaser using a compelling question. Highlight the importance of the issue. At the same time, stress its impact. Show the reader that it's closer to home than he may realize. Follow that with an urgent note for him to "look inside" for details.

Offer helpful information

Let's face it. We live in a how-to society. It's a world where people feed on self-help guides, instructional books, and "easy ways to do something" articles. Well, reporters are aware of this. They know that "tips" are good attention-getters. For that reason, we see teasers that promise us solutions to all of our problems.

Example: *"Do you have chronic back pain? Tune in at 11 and discover five ways you can prevent it."*

People are literally drawn to headlines that promise useful information in a numbered format.

People are literally drawn to headlines that promise useful information in a numbered format. "Five ways to prevent back pain" will get more attention than "Preventing back pain." There's something about the numbers, the "Five ways."

Letter-opening copy can sometimes be a challenge to write. It can even be intimidating. Yet, with the right tools, some patience, and a dose of TV news reporting, it can also be fun. Even more, it can be profitable!

2. The Letter

Of all the items included in a direct mail package, the letter is undoubtedly the most important. It is the engine that moves the car, the muscle that lifts the weight, and the argument that makes the sale. It can stand with or without a flier. It can sell even without a lift note.

Because of the important role it plays, it is absolutely essential to write and rewrite, polish and revise, until you've made it the best that it can be.

A letter can be effective as a one-page job, as in lead generation packages. However, when you are selling directly and you need immediate action, longer is generally better. In other words, a two-page letter will out-pull a single page; a four-page letter will out-pull two pages; and a six-page letter will usually out-perform four pages. Remember the saying, "The more you tell, the more you sell."

Unlike the flier or brochure, the letter gives you space to make a complete sales pitch. It allows room to tell your story in detail. It permits short sentences, bullet points, long paragraphs, underlined words, bold type, and even handwritten notes in the margin.

The best letters are those written in a personal, conversational style, just like you're writing to a friend. Instead of speaking to a crowd, you address only a single person. For this reason, your letter should be filled with second-person references, as in "you." You are also permitted to use "I"—the first person.

To make your letter readable and persuasive, simply apply some of the same techniques used in advertising. With this in mind, consider the following.

The best letters are those written in a personal, conversational style, just like you're writing to a friend.

Begin with a strong headline

Some businesses use letterhead with logos that blanket the top of the page. This, I believe, is a mistake. "If you have a logo or design for your business, do not use it in the sales letter unless it is truly relevant to what you are offering," advises copywriter Sonny Bliss.

"You are not selling your business name, or logo, you are selling benefits that the buyer will realize if he buys your product or service."

Remember, readers are interested in one thing: "What's in it for me?" Therefore it is best to begin the page with a powerful, hard-hitting headline.

Are there exceptions? Of course. "There is only one exception to this rule," noted copywriter Joe Vitale. "When you personalize your letter, the 'Dear (whoever)' opening becomes your headline."

Vitale notes there are few headlines more effective than the reader's own name. Even so, he says, "The headline is the most important part of your letter. Spend nearly all of your time on it."

The opening sentence or lead paragraph

The purpose of the headline is to catch attention and draw the reader into the contents of the letter. Ideally, it will compel them to read the first sentence. Once they reach this point, the first sentence piques their curiosity, creates desire, and pulls them into the body of the letter.

How is that done?

Always shoot your big gun first. Open with a loud bang—with the most important benefit or idea you can present in a short sentence. Write a short, snappy sentence that appeals to the reader's interest. This could be in the form of a question, a provocative statement, a startling fact, summary of a problem or solution, or a major benefit. Keep the reader's self-interest in mind.

The body of the letter

Now that you have the reader's attention and you've created a desire, the next step is to begin telling your story with the intent of creating interest in your message. You can do that by highlighting the benefits (not just the features) of your product or service, and by building a case for what you can do for the reader.

Tell a story that the reader can relate to. Mention a news item that the reader can identify with. Simply write the way you talk.

*F*ill your letter with believable facts, statistics, and testimonials. Bring on the endorsements.

Fill your letter with believable facts, statistics, and testimonials. Bring on the endorsements. Use illustrations or anecdotes that drive your message home. Use subheads throughout the letter, preferably after every two or three paragraphs.

Feel free to underline important sentences. Make important words bold. Use all caps for words or sentences that you want to stand out.

The offer and guarantee

After you have made a case for your message, be sure to state your offer. Tell the reader what he or she must do immediately in order to receive your product. Then provide a guarantee that can't be beat.

Select one that's not used by your competitor. Create one that removes all doubt about your customer's satisfaction. Use one that shows your commitment to the offer.

The call to action

Once the offer is stated clearly, and precisely, deliver your "call to action" by telling the reader to "Act NOW!" If there's a deadline, then state it boldly. If there are extra benefits or a premium incentive, state it boldly. In other words, let the reader know what he or she will lose (or gain) by failing to "Act Today!"

The P.S.

Once these ingredients are in place, you have one last chance in the letter to drive your point home. I'm speaking here of the "P.S." You may be surprised to know that the "P.S." is often the second—and last—element that people read when they scan a letter. So use this to your advantage by either highlighting a benefit already covered in the letter, or by announcing an extra benefit. Some copywriters use the "P.S." to restate a deadline. In such a case, it becomes a reminder or "Your final warning."

"Why do copywriters who charge upwards to $15,000 to write a sales letter and have weeks to draft it always use a PS?" asks Joe Vitale. "They are always read. Always."

3. The Flyer or Brochure

Although the letter is the workhorse of direct mail, it can be well-supported by a flyer or brochure. "Other pieces of support literature that amplify the selling points, illustrate the product or service, or provide technical information, may be needed," according to Sonny Bliss. "Supplement the letter with a brochure or product sheet if necessary, and if you do, mention it in the body of the letter."

Although the letter is the workhorse of direct mail, it can be well-supported by a flyer or brochure.

As a sales tool, the flier gives you the chance to play with color, format, and other creative styles. It is the place to bring on the bells and whistles, all in an attempt to support the letter, your sales message, and bring the reader to action.

A good flier can be of any design and length. But whether it's one page or multiple pages, it also must have the sales elements of a good advertisement. Strong headlines, graphics, bullet points, boxed statements, highlighted benefits, all must be organized and presented in a way that will move the reader to action.

Testimonials, like the headlines, should hold prominent places. The same is true for the offer, the guarantee, and call to action. These elements should stand out and be easily seen with only a quick glance at the document.

4. The Response Card

Next to the letter, the response card may well be the most important item in your direct mail package. It is the final step of a long journey—the last gesture before closing the deal.

For those reasons, it makes sense to develop a card (or form) that really works. A good order form (I prefer the term "response card") does what its name implies—it generates response. Such a card is practical and easy to follow.

Most marketing professionals know the value of a good response card. But many seem to struggle with both the copy and the design—two crucial elements that make a response card work.

Whenever you're working on a mailing, try to keep this single point in mind: A sense of urgency and excitement must flow easily from the letter to the response card. Both pieces should ooze with the same passion and sincerity.

Now with that said, here are some quick tips to get you started with writing effective copy.

Be clear about your instructions

In his excellent book, *The Complete Book of Model Fund-Raising Letters* (Paramus, N.J.; Prentice Hall, 1995), Roland Kuniholm wrote: "Your letter may motivate someone to give. But if that prospective donor looks at the gift response form and is confused or unsure as to how to respond all the good effort on the letter is lost."

What a powerful truth to remember! It's been said that if you give someone a chance to misunderstand you, they will do just that.

Strive to be clear. Spell out exactly what you want prospects to do. You may start with the letter by telling them what to do with the enclosed response card. Then at the top of the card, you can tell them to "clip and mail."

Use a powerful headline or title

What do you call your response device: A response card? Order form? Donor certificate? Enrollment Form?

Every response card should have some type of heading that lets the prospect know what he or she is holding. "Always use a headline on the order card," said direct marketer Ted Nicholas. "This tends to create a feeling that it's an important document. Many mailers omit a headline, which is a mistake."

Restate your purpose

Your response card is your last chance to make your pitch. So drive your point home by restating what you underscored in your letter.

Your response card is your last chance to make your pitch. So drive your point home by restating what you underscored in your letter. Simply remind the prospect of the need and the urgency of your request.

Some writers grab attention with a "Dear John" opening at the top of their response cards. The opening reads like a letter.

Example: *"Dear John, I want to cut the fat and get in shape. Please send me ..."*

You see, in that simple opening, the purpose is noted. It builds on what was previously stated in the letter.

Use involvement devices

Use the classic YES! and No boxes that must be checked by the prospect.

When writing, use the YES! box as an affirmation tool. It's a way to get the prospect to agree with you and your offer.

Example: ❏ YES! I want to have the best vacation of my life …

With the No box, give the prospect a way to purchase at a later time.

Example: ❏ No. I do not need this service at this time. Please contact me in

_____.

Give options

Depending on the purpose of your mailing, you could probably give prospects a number of ways to make a purchase. Give them the option of paying by check, credit card, by phone, or through your web site.

When you set out to design your response card, think of ways to make it stand out from the rest of the package. Create an image that would motivate prospects to pick up your card, read it, sign it, and send it in with a check. If you like, you can borrow ideas from other businesses.

Study them and take note of the many designs you may choose from. In the meantime, you may consider these ideas:

Depending on the purpose of your mailing, you could probably give prospects a number of ways to make a purchase.

Use a different color

Over the years, I've come across a number of direct mail packages that used the same color of paper and ink for each of their enclosures: The letter, response card, and brochure were all white or some other color.

When you opened such a package, somehow the single color made you feel you simply had one long letter and nothing else. Now, I'm sure that design has worked for some groups, but to me, it has some built-in weaknesses. For one thing, it downplays the need for options, something prospects need. When everything in a mailing looks the same, nothing stands out. The result? Prospects will likely read a little and put the rest aside.

However, with options (as with different colors), they are likely to check out each enclosure. In some cases, they'll glance at each element before reading the letter.

Make it look like a coupon

Does your response card look like a response card? Or does it look like a page from your letter?

Some marketers have turned page three or four of their letters into response forms. But I think it's a mistake. Remember, people have a compulsion to clip coupons. They feel compelled to fill in order blanks. To encourage that, certain graphics must be applied.

At the very least, use a strong border line (or a certificate border) around your copy, giving it the image of a coupon. Another method is to use a perforated dotted line. In some cases, you may want to use a different texture of paper. Try something of a heavier grade than your letter.

Test different sizes

Some response cards work best in a full-page (letter size) format, while others work in a smaller format. In most cases, the size you choose will be determined by the amount of copy (and options) you use to get a response.

My rule of thumb is simple: Lots of copy needs lots of space. Little copy needs little space. Whichever you choose, just remember to use type that's big enough for easy reading. In other words, your prospect should not have to squint and strain in order to read and fill in your response card. Choose a size that makes its user friendly.

5. The Lift Note and Business Reply Envelope

Research shows that mailings can obtain a better response rate by including a lift note.

The lift note is designed to do as its name implies: lift response. Research shows that mailings can obtain a better response rate by including a lift note. Not surprisingly, this tiny message, printed as a letter on a small sheet of colored paper, is now a popular feature of direct mail. Generally, it is folded and includes a headline with a brief message that urges the reader to make a decision. Perhaps you've seen the ones with the headline, "Read this only if you've decided not to respond." In short, it's another last-ditch attempt to reel the prospect in. Done well, it makes the reader think twice before casting the mail aside.

Whether you use a lift note is up to you. A mailing can be successful without it. However, it may be worth the effort to at least test it for results. The same is true of the business reply envelope (BRE). For your first efforts, it may be a good idea to use the BRE, as this makes it easy for the prospect to respond. And in direct mail, the easier it is for a prospect to respond, the greater your chances are of getting the order.

The focus of this section has been on direct mail in the traditional sense. But keep in mind that direct mail includes other types of advertisements that rely on the delivery of mail. This includes postcards, newsletters, self-mailers, mega-logs, magazines, shoppers, etc. While all of the other methods are useful, they tend to work best as a supplement to the traditional package that consists of the letter. So when you begin your campaign, plan to put most of your time and effort into the letter (along with its envelope teaser, flier, and response card). Once you have that in place, you may then consider the use of postcards or other communications to support your primary marketing package.

Chapter 11

7 Quick Tips for Better Lead Generation:

A Checklist for Attracting Prospects and Getting All the Leads You'll Ever Need

ARE YOU PLEASED WITH THE NUMBER OF LEADS YOU'RE GETTING through your direct-mail package? What about the calls you get after placing an ad? Or the response rates of your postcard or e-mail campaigns?

If you would like to improve both the number of leads and their quality, then take a look at the following check list. Whether you have a letter, a card deck, an ad, or a brochure, this check list will help you to polish and invigorate your sales copy. Use it to breathe life into tired, worn-out marketing documents.

Perhaps it's worth mentioning that most of the following tips are similar (some, the same) as those used for print advertisements. That's OK, because advertising is advertising no matter what medium you use. The thing to keep in mind is that tips and ideas, though similar (and seemingly repetitive), actually work. In fact, they've been used successfully by advertising professionals for over 100 years.

That said, let's get started!

1. Focus on the prospects

As noted elsewhere in this guide, a common mistake made by many businesses is to focus on themselves—and not on their prospects. To do that is to violate one of the basic rules of marketing.

Instead of thinking how great your products or services are, think of how they will benefit your prospects. Instead of focusing on your company's strengths, focus on what your company can do for your prospects.

Never stop asking: "What's in it for *them*?" After all, your prospects are asking: "What's in it for *me*?"

2. Get attention

Before you can turn prospects into good, qualified leads, you need to get their attention. You must stop them in their tracks and compel them to read your document.

How is that done? You guessed it. By using a striking headline or a compelling piece of art. Engage the prospects. Highlight a free offer or use the prospects' names. You may also offer a challenging question.

Getting attention, as you have learned, means standing out and sounding off. You don't get it by whispering. You get it by shouting. For that reason, use headlines and art that leap off the page. Be bold and daring. Don't worry about being cute. Strive, instead, to be noticed ... to be heard ... and seen!

3. Identify the problem

In business-to-business marketing, most products are created to meet a need or solve a problem.

In business-to-business marketing, most products are created to meet a need or solve a problem. For that reason, you should remind the prospects of their problem and what it's costing them. Be direct and yet friendly in pointing out the need that should be met. Use images and language your prospects can understand.

In other words, bring on the hurt and pour on the pain. Where possible, use words to paint a vivid picture of the struggles your prospect has. Let him or her know that you fully understand what they're going through. And that something must be done about it.

4. Offer a solution

After making your prospects sweat, you are then ready to give them some relief. It's found in your product or service.

Simply make a smooth transition from the description of their problem and lead into your product or service as the solution. Show how your product can either fill their need or solve their problem.

5. Give proof

Today, we live in a skeptical world where bragging doesn't mean what it used to. It's no longer enough to say your product is the best or it can fix a certain problem. People want proof. It's "Show me the money or show me nothing."

People want proof. It's "Show me the money or show me nothing."

When you mention your product or service as a solution, quickly support it with testimonials or a list of clients. Include facts or survey results.

6. Call for action

Leads don't just occur; they come when people are told what to do. So don't hesitate to tell your prospects what you want them to do and when. Instead of saying, "We look forward to hearing from you," say something like: "Call today for your FREE ..." Or, you might say: "Please fill in the enclosed order form and mail it today. There is no cost or obligation."

7. Give an incentive

People need a reason to respond. You can induce action by offering a free gift or a tight deadline.

Chapter 12

7 Important Facts About Using Radio:
Warnings and Advice to Save You Money

IN HIS DELIGHTFUL BOOK, HEY WHIPPLE, SQUEEZE THIS, *LUKE SULLIVAN* opens a chapter with this interesting statement:

"It is one of the great mysteries of advertising. Most radio is, well, it's not very good."

He goes on to say that radio advertising is not popular among many advertisers. And that for some people, he included, it can be scary.

Indeed, it appears that of all the media outlets available to small businesses, radio is at the bottom. While it seems to work for some, there are many others that have not been able to use it in a profitable manner. Perhaps this is due to its technical challenges or maybe a dwindling audience. For whatever reason, radio is not the first medium that comes to mind when you think of advertising.

That being said, I should note that the purpose of this section is not to provide details about the technical aspects of radio, but rather to offer general ideas on the use of this medium along with tips for writing direct-response commercials.

7 Things You Should Know About Using Radio

Radio may or may not be a viable marketing tool for your business. But if you want to try it, and perhaps test a few ideas, keep the following points in mind:

1. Radio is "theater of the mind"

Its strength is in the use of words, music, and sound effects to create vivid images in the minds of its listeners. Since photos are reserved for print, and video images are reserved for TV, your words and sounds must work extra hard to grab attention and move your audience to action.

You can't show the picture of ice cubes, but you can describe the image and provide the sound of cubes falling into a glass. It's the same with food. You can't show the picture of a burger, but you can describe the charcoal flavor and provide the sound of it sizzling on a grill. In the case of a health remedy or weight-loss product, you substitute visual images by describing the problem through the pain and suffering of a character. The character discovers your product and finds relief. All this must be dramatized through the use of words and sound effects.

2. A good voice-over begins with a good script or "pitch"

An effective radio script has three parts: First, it has a beginning section that provides a context for the offer. Second, it has a middle section that provides the reasons to act or to buy. Third, it has a call to action, in which listeners are invited to make a phone call or visit a particular site.

In writing your script, be sure to think of your audience. Consider their language, their habits, their music, and all the things you would say to them in a face-to-face meeting. In other words, the voice must fit the prospect: You don't communicate with a country music lover by speaking the language of a rapper.

The voice must fit the prospect: You don't communicate with a country music lover by speaking the language of a rapper.

3. A good radio script is tight and concise

You have neither the space nor the time to play around. For a 30-second spot, you're allowed up to 72 words max, and up to 130 words for a 60-second spot.

Remember the importance of headlines in print? In radio, the headline consists of the first words that are spoken. They should grab the attention of your listeners and convince them to hear the rest of your message.

Examples:

"Have you been turned down again for a car loan? We can help! Call...."

"Are you tired of people pushing your around? Then do something about it. Call...."

After leading with your "headline," state a key benefit and make a call for action. It's that simple.

4. Direct-response copy must be simple and direct

Copywriter Peter A. Buckhard has noted that direct-response copy for radio can be a challenge, but in order to be effective, it must be clear and direct. "Give people something they can use NOW," he said. "No music. No funny ha! ha! The standard approach addresses a problem with a direct solution."

To illustrate his point, Buckhard gave this example:

"Oh, NO! Itchy, flaky dandruff again! Isn't it time to get rid of itchy dandruff once and for all? Call 1-800-NO-ITCH6 for our free..."

5. Humor is OK but not a requirement for a good commercial

Here you must exercise caution. Why? It's easy to get carried away with jokes. What you think is funny may be a dud to your audience. "Humor is the first fork in the road taken by every copywriter in the nation on every radio job they get," noted Luke Sullivan. "I don't blame them. It's fun to laugh, and radio seems to beg for it." Yet, Sullivan advised, "If you want to stand out in this medium, try something other than humor. It may not work, but you should at least try it."

6. The music must not overpower the message

Music is a great tool for enhancing a sales message, but overdone, your audience will remember the music and not the message. So whether you use songs, jingles, or plain music, make sure it is second fiddle to the copy. Or, in the words of Guerrilla Marketing Expert Jay Conrad Levinson, "Be sure the music enhances and doesn't interfere with your message."

In terms of formats, radio gives you a choice in how the music is played. It can be used in the background of your message or in the foreground. Whichever method you choose, ensure that it's the type of music that resonates with your audience.

Of course, there may be times when you go for the shock value in order to get attention. In this case, you can experiment with something that will raise eyebrows without offending.

7. Repetition is a key factor to inducing response

As noted elsewhere in this book, repetition is an important feature in all types of marketing and advertising endeavors. In some cases it is absolutely essential to driving your message home. Since many listeners will hear your message while driving, you need to repeat key points so they can remember them or have time to jot them down. In this case you can repeat a certain benefit, date and time of an event, or the phone number to call.

It's worth a try. There's little doubt that when it's done well, radio can indeed be an effective marketing tool for smart marketers. But will it work for your business? Are your prospects and customers fans of radio? Do they spend much time on the road? Do they enjoy listening to music or talk radio?

Your decision to use this medium will depend on your answers to the above questions. Of course, your budget will also play a role in your decision. While radio may not be a fit for all small businesses, it is worth a try, a simple test, to see who's listening. Experiment and see what happens!

Since many listeners will hear your message while driving, you need to repeat key points so they can remember them or have time to jot them down.

Chapter 13

15 Critical Facts About Using the Web:

Strategic Tips for Advertising on the Internet

I F YOU LISTEN TO THE HYPE PROMOTED BY THE SO-CALLED INTERNET MAR-keting gurus, you'd think the Internet is uncharted territory with advertising secrets that only the gurus possess. For a few thousand dollars (or hundreds, depending on the product), these gurus will reveal "for the first time ever" their secrets of success.

Unfortunately, when you look for evidence of their success, you find that they made their riches only by telling other marketers how to get rich.

Copywriters understandably have different views on writing for the Internet. For instance, Daniel Levis, editor and publisher of *Web Marketing Advisor*, believes there are many more similarities than there are differences between the print and online copy requirements. Bob Bly contends that whether you market online or offline, copy is still king. He writes: "Just because a person buys online doesn't change the persuasion process. If he needs the facts to make a decision, he needs them regardless of whether he is ordering from a paper mailing or a web site."

Of course, the use of any medium might require some adjustment in strategy and copy, or other variable. That's a given. In the case of Internet advertising, copy is most effective when it's written for people on the move—the web surfers. Therefore, copy is best if it is short or at least half as long as printed text, according to Kathy Henning, who writes extensively on online communication.

Truth be told, Internet marketing requires some of the same advertising concepts and techniques that have been around for over a hundred years. The reason is that human nature has not changed. Technology and media outlets have changed and will no doubt continue to do so, but the basic needs and desires of human nature will remain the same. However, that is not to say that the Internet does not present any challenges, or for that matter, opportunities.

Truth be told, Internet marketing requires some of the same advertising concepts and techniques that have been around for over a hundred years.

E-Commerce Is In Full Bloom

Like mail order of yesteryear, many a small business has been created through the use of the Internet. Many have started on a shoe-string budget, selling everything from books on Amazon.com or specialty items on eBay. Some have used the Internet to supplement their income, while others use it as an essential marketing tool for traditional businesses.

Author Michael Corbett has stated that when it comes to advertising, "any medium will work if you know how to work the medium." Yet, he also suggested that the jury is still out on the use of the Internet for local business owners. What he bases this on, I'm not sure. But over the last few years, particularly since 2000, I have personally witnessed a growing number of small businesses that use the Internet as a viable medium in promoting their products and services.

What about your business? Are you currently reaching customers through the web? Have you tried it and given up? Or are you a reluctant newbie who wants to play it safe before launching out into the deep?

Actually, it doesn't matter whether you're an Internet old-timer or you're just starting out, it would be helpful to get a basic sense of what works—and what doesn't work—before you invest in the effort.

Begin by determining your purpose in cyberspace, then grow your business accordingly. Do you merely want a web site that serves as a press kit or information storehouse? Or do you want to sell products and generate leads?

Obviously, you have the freedom to choose. That's the beauty of the Internet: It provides you with scores of possibilities that are limited only by your imagination.

But let's face it: Not every web site is meant to sell. For instance, some companies use the web strictly for public relations. They have no interest in directly selling products or services. For them, the web is like a giant resume or portfolio of sorts. It provides readers with vital information such as background, history, goals, mission, and photographs about the respective company.

Several marketers use their web sites primarily as a way to position them as the leading authority in their field. In addition to highlighting their success, they include pages listing books, recommended resources, and free articles on their topic. If they travel as speakers or trainers, they include their itinerary.

Several marketers use their web sites primarily as a way to position them as the leading authority in their field.

The important thing here is to think of your audience. Put yourself in their place and then ask yourself what you'd want to know about your type of business. What would you want to see on a web page? How could this business help you achieve your goals or prevent you from suffering pain or a personal loss?

Keep these questions in mind as you plan your Internet marketing campaign.

Next, select a domain that speaks to your audience. Will it carry your personal name, as in "JohnDoe.com" or your business name, "Quickservice.com"? You also have the option of simply focusing on a solution, as in "EmergencyRoadService.com" or "sellyourhome.com."

Another method is to focus on a problem, as in "Goingbald.com" or "Tiredoffat.com."

When selecting a name for your web site, consider one that's easy to pronounce, easy to spell, and easy to remember. And, as you've learned about advertising, consider a name that offers a benefit or addresses a problem or felt need of your prospects.

A short time ago I learned of a young businessman who was chided by a copywriter because he wanted to use his name as a domain.

"It's OK, if you're well known," the copywriter said. "But since you're just starting out, it would be a mistake."

While I certainly understand the copywriter, I have to disagree. Why? A fundamental rule in marketing and self-promotion is to keep your name before the audience you want to reach. This is the first step in becoming well known. Although your name may be unknown today, repeated exposure will catapult you into the minds of your market and soon enough, you will have all the recognition—and business—that you desire.

A Common Problem in Web Marketing

I'll never forget one interview I had for a copywriting assignment. The director of marketing was eager to launch a web site that sells software for tax professionals. He wanted to know about my experience in writing business-to-business copy for the web. Well, at the time, I had only a few sample pages for consumer and business-to-business markets. Yet, confident of my writing abilities, I commenced to explain there were no major differences between print and online advertising copy.

"Actually," said the manager. "There's a big difference."

As he explained his point, it became clear that he was caught up with graphics, flash, and all the bells and whistles of new technology. Unfortunately, he knew little about writing copy that gets results.

This manager's ideas about Internet advertising are rather common, especially among inexperienced marketers. Too often the excitement of new technology seems to overwhelm them, and in some cases, blind them to the things that really matter.

15 Things You Should Know About Using the Internet

So that you can avoid having the wrong ideas about the use of the Internet, I have included a few important facts for your consideration.

1. Web sites allow for 24-hour business

This is a great advantage and the benefits are obvious. It allows you to compete with bigger stores that are open around the clock. Since you don't have the staff or the money for such a feat, you can let your web site do the work for you. Not only is it cheaper, but it's also easier.

Think about it. While you are sleeping, customers can visit your site and browse your offerings. They can also place orders. Even more, the web site allows you to reach people on both the local and national level.

When creating your web site, remember to keep it simple and easy to read and follow. Include a large benefit-driven headline at the top of the page. Don't forget to add some type of free offer, such as an e-zine, in order to hold on to the customers.

When creating your web site, remember to keep it simple and easy to read and follow.

2. Ads may be used to boost traffic

Retailers have known for years that advertising in the local print media will drive traffic to their stores. Fortunately, the same thing can happen with web sites. By placing small ads in selected publications (online and offline), you can announce your benefits and draw customers to your web site. This process works best when you have an enticing offer. In other words, reward the customer for visiting. Otherwise, he or she might take a quick look and move on.

3. Landing pages are essential for increasing response

"Landing pages" are short Internet-based forms that are generally used to explain the offer that has been advertised in another medium. Typically, customers will see your ad or read your e-mail and click on a hot link for more information. When they click on this link, they "land" on another page. This landing page, which may be short with only a couple of paragraphs, or longer, is where you'll find the rest of the story, so to speak. This page has a mechanism for the customer to fill in his or her information and submit a response—or place an order.

4. E-zines can be used to build customer loyalty

The "e-zine," also called "e-Mag" or "e-Newsletter," is one of the most inexpensive marketing tools available to the small business person. It can be of practically any length and may be published weekly, monthly, quarterly, or as often as you like. You can use it to promote special offers, discounts, new products or services, etc.

What's great about this tool is that you can publish it without the cost of print, postage, and mailing. You can rent a list of names or build your own list. Even more, you can sell ad space to your subscribers or other businesses (noncompeting, of course).

Publishing an e-zine is ideal for keeping in touch with your customers. It's a sure-fire way to build loyalty and thereby increase sales.

Publishing an e-zine is ideal for keeping in touch with your customers. It's a sure-fire way to build loyalty and thereby increase sales.

5. Special offers may be used to collect names

A good mailing list (of customers or prospects) is like money in the bank. It enables you to contact customers on your own terms and without the cost of advertising.

One way to develop a good list is through special offers on your web site (or in your e-zine). To receive the offers, which could be anything from a special report, coupon, or e-book, the person must provide an e-mail address and/or mailing address along with a phone number.

You must then save this information and use it to keep in touch with your customers.

6. A Sig line is a no-cost way to promote your business

The "sig line," which is short for "signature line," is that line of copy below your name in an e-mail, and postings in a discussion group. You can use three to six lines to provide your title, business, service, and contact information that includes your web address.

Many marketers use a slogan that highlights their USP (Unique Selling Proposition), followed by a hot link to their web site. Example: "Mary Doe Realty—Selling your home at the speed of light." This has proven to be effective. Others use a headline in the form of a question:

"Would you like to lose seven pounds in the next two weeks?"

In short, the sig line should be viewed as a mini-ad that gives you exposure and generates leads for little or no cost.

7. E-mails are great for announcing special offers

This common feature of the Internet is too often neglected by some businesses. When I lived in Baltimore, Maryland, I spent a lot of time visiting bookstores. Of all that I visited, only one asked for my e-mail address. The store was Greenleaf Christian Bookstore.

Periodically, the store sends me e-mails about upcoming events, coupons, new books, and special discounts. Because of this, when I think of certain Christian books, I tend to think of this particular store. Even though I have relocated from Baltimore, I still receive the e-mails and, I might add, I am always delighted to see the offers.

What about your business? Do you collect the e-mail addresses of your customers? Do you use the e-mail addresses to keep them abreast of your offerings? Do you contact them on holidays?

8. E-books may be used as premiums and products

If you want to position yourself as an expert in your field, then write a few e-books on a topic that will interest your prospects and customers. The most effective titles are those that provide how-to information or timely research. Unlike books that are traditionally printed, e-books are less expensive to produce and they do not have to be long. Actually, they can be as short as

26 pages and promoted as "Special Reports." Or they may be as long as you need them to be.

Once you have created one, consider offering it as a premium to prospects or customers who try your products. Later, after you have written several, you may want to include a selling price and market them as you would any other product.

9. Blogging is a creative way to show your personal side

Although blogging is great for sharing personal episodes from your life, it also is a way to share your opinion and provide helpful information in a timely manner.

This method of communication also allows you to build a following of readers who look to you as the expert on a particular topic. Although blogging is great for sharing personal episodes from your life, it also is a way to share your opinion and provide helpful information in a timely manner. Beyond these factors, blogging may be interactive, in that readers can comment on your writing. This can lead to solid relationships among your customer base.

10. A discussion group is good for building a customer community

In business conversations, you often hear comments about the need for repeat business. There's always talk about doing something to "keep customers coming back." Well, thanks to the Internet, this is possible through the ever popular forums known as "discussion groups." This aspect of the web provides a meeting place for people with common interests. Fortunately, it's also a way for a small business to develop a customer community. A number of small businesses have done just that. They include Degreeinfo.com, Writersweekly.com, Absolutewrite.com, and ATX/Kleinrock, among others.

Note: *One downside of this feature is the time it takes to moderate the discussion.*

11. Discussion groups are great for exposure

Depending on the nature of your business, discussion groups can be an easy way to meet new prospects and generate interest in your products or services. Since overt advertising is frowned upon in discussion groups, the best way to promote without spamming is to simply include a good sig line that mentions your title or business, along with a link to your web site.

In most cases you will gravitate to the discussion groups that share your interests. When members ask questions that relate to your interests, you can answer them as an authority without any sales talk. Over time you will gain the respect of the members who may seek you out for business.

12. Writing articles is a sure-fire way to extend your visibility

Since the culture of the Internet is all about "Free," providing free articles to e-zines is an effective method for generating publicity. In addition to providing solid information that is useful to your prospects, the articles position you as an authority. Of course, each article should include a resource box at the end. This box is the "About the Author" section that provides your background information and the URL for your web site.

In the June 1, 2006, issue of *Publishing Poynters*, Dan Poynter featured a tip on this topic by public relations specialist, Pam Lontos. Although her focus is on the print media, the same ideas apply to e-publications.

Here's what she wrote:

> Imagine that you get an article into an industry or trade magazine that goes to 80,000 people. If you were to do a mailer, at two dollars a piece—which is an inexpensive mailer for printing, postage, and everything—and you sent that to 80,000 people, it would cost you $160,000. If you got into a magazine like *Cosmopolitan* that would go to two million people, instead of a mailer that cost two dollars per piece, you would get FOUR MILLION DOLLARS worth of publicity!

> What's more, publication has greater credibility than a mailing, because the media source is quoting you as an expert, or publishing your "expert" article, not yet another self-promoting piece of direct mail. So it's easier, cheaper, and gives you more benefit!

13. Sharing links is an effective way to partner with other businesses

It's been said, "There's strength in numbers." If this is true, then you can benefit by drawing on the resources of other businesses that use the Internet. While this can be done in a number of ways, one effective way is to simply include links on your web site that direct customers to other noncompeting businesses. Of course, you would first ask for permission and at the same time, you would ask the other businesses to include links to your web site.

To get the most out of this process, you'd want to mention a product or service on one of your pages and place it under a heading like, "Recommended

Resource." One marketer includes a whole list of "Recommended Vendors," and another features a whole page of "Recommended Printers."

Ideally you want to include links that complement your business.

14. "FREE" is the magic word in cyberspace

B ecause Internet users have come to expect free information in this form of communication, it makes sense to accommodate them and provide them with more than they expect.

Remember, when prospects visit your web site, they need a reason to return, as well as a reason to recommend your site to others. Because Internet users have come to expect free information in this form of communication, it makes sense to accommodate them and provide them with more than they expect. This is accomplished by making your web site a one-stop shop that offers loads of free products that will help your prospects achieve their goals.

What type of products? Include a list of free how-to articles, free research reports, a list of vendors, recommended books, recommended e-zines, photographs, product samples, e-books, a free consultation, etc.

15. Promoting your web site is an unending venture

Once you have your web site in place, and your products and services are ready for promotion, it is time to start promoting the web site in order to build traffic. Although advertising should be included, your efforts should consist of other channels as well.

Where to start? Make sure that your web address is featured on all relevant documents, including business cards, letterhead, press releases, receipts, thank-you cards, pens, mugs, calendars, postcards, shopping bags, envelopes, etc.

This list of "15 facts" about using the Internet to promote your business should give you an idea of what it takes to promote your enterprise in cyberspace. You will no doubt experiment and discover a few things not covered here. That's a good thing. But remember that whatever you do in marketing, always keep it simple and test before making a big investment. Do this and your Internet journey should be a lot smoother, more fun, and, of course, more profitable!

Chapter 14

20 Ideas for Saturation and Visibility:
Creative Underground Ways to Promote Your Message

WHEN YOUR PROSPECTS HAVE A NEED, DO THEY THINK OF YOU— or your business? When your customers have a goal, do they think of you? Or do they first think of your competition?

As the manager or owner of a small business, you want your enterprise to be well known and easily accessible to clients, prospects, and customers. When they have a need, you want them to think of you—and not your competition.

Yet, bringing prospects to this point is not always easy. In fact, it's not unreasonable to remember "The Rule of Seven." This phrase, coined by Dr. Jeffrey Lant, suggests that on average, a person must be contacted at least seven times with a sales message before he or she responds. If this is true (and I believe it is), a small businessperson must draw on a host of resources in order to drive a message home. In short, this calls for unceasing saturation and visibility, which relies on the repetition of your message in numerous outlets. To accomplish this, you have to advertise your message repeatedly in as many ways as possible. Your advertising should also be supplemented by free publicity.

20 Ideas for Saturation and Visibility

Following is a list of 20 ideas that will help you to generate exposure and sear your sales message into the minds of your audience.

1. Use product ads

You've seen them. Probably hundreds of times. A business places its name and sales message on all types of products, including pens, mugs, calendars, paper clips, t-shirts, book marks, key chains, etc. These items are then given away to prospects and customers as "freebies."

Pens are a favorite for drug companies. Whenever I have a doctor's visit, I pick up a handful of "medical" pens dropped off by a sales representative.

There seems to be a growing number of companies that provide promotional products. Do a search on the Internet and you can view their catalogs.

2. Use alternative methods

It won't hurt to be creative in choosing a place to advertise your business. Back in the days when smoking was popular, wise marketers printed ads on the covers of matchboxes. Today a number of other methods are used for sales messages. They include: bumper stickers, movie tickets, grocery receipts, gas pumps, and table mats (at local restaurants).

Just recently I purchased groceries at a local store and was pleased to see that the backside of my receipt was covered with ads from local businesses. I went out to the parking lot, near the store's gas station, and there on the pumps I saw other sales messages. It brought a smile to my face as I thought, "If they don't get you in the store, they'll get you at the pump."

3. Write press releases

Press releases should be used regularly to promote some aspect of your business.

The press release is the work-horse of the public relations industry. Press releases should be used regularly to promote some aspect of your business. Simply identify various news angles about your product or service, or even your employees, write up a one-page press release, and submit it to newspapers and appropriate magazines and newsletters. This news could cover any number of topics, including the opening of new business, promotion of an employee, purchase of new property, publication of a book, achievements and granting of awards, etc.

4. Write letters to the editor

One of the most widely read sections of a newspaper and magazine is the editorial page where "letters to the editor" are printed. Do you have an opinion on a particular news topic? Can you provide expert knowledge? If so, then write a letter and include your business name and title. Do this often enough and readers may ask you to run for office.

5. Hit the speaking circuit

Begin by contacting the local Chamber of Commerce and inquire about groups needing public speakers. Every community has its share of social and business clubs and they often need speakers for breakfast and lunch meetings. Consider the Rotary Club or the Optimist Club, among others. Speaking before these groups will make you popular among the leaders of the community.

6. Donate to worthy causes

What are the needs in your community? Can you contribute in some way? Perhaps the local school needs computers or the library needs shelves, or the Easter Seal Society needs funding or the Girl Scouts needs uniforms. Just take a look and determine where your business can make a donation.

7. Publish a newsletter

This is can be a small one- or two-page letter in print or an e-zine. Use it to keep your prospects and customers informed. Share news and upcoming events, including special discounts or speaking engagements. Alert them to new products and share holiday greetings. Publish bi-weekly, monthly, or as often as you like.

8. Use postcards announcing "breaking news"

Postcards are great for sending out reminders or for delivering last-minute news. Besides being easy to design, they are also inexpensive to print and mail. Use them for special occasions, holidays, and birthdays.

9. Write a column about your expertise

This is a proven way to establish your reputation as an expert in your field. A good column only has to be about 500 words for newspapers and e-zines. They may be a bit longer for trade publications. If you have a lot of ideas, particularly how-to information for your audience, then contact the local paper or the appropriate newsletter or magazine and ask if you can write a column for their publication. Provide a title for the column and include your resume or information on your background. Let them know if the column will be a weekly (for newspapers) or a monthly (for magazines). When the column is accepted, be sure to include details about your background and business at the end of each column.

10. Build a mailing list

Make a determined effort to collect the names and addresses of prospects and customers. Then use this information as a means to contact them regularly throughout the year.

Make a determined effort to collect the names and addresses of prospects and customers. Then use this information as a means to contact them regularly throughout the year. Through letters, postcards, or a newsletter, you can use this mailing list to "upsell" current customers or reel in the reluctant prospects. Use of the mailing list also saves you money that would have been spent on advertising.

11. Use direct mail

Direct mail is simply delivering your sales message directly to your audience by mail. This method is great for reaching prospects and customers alike. The ideal direct-mail package contains copy—a teaser—on the outer envelope, a sales letter, a response card, and sometimes a flier and lift note. Whether you want to generate leads or make direct sales, direct mail is an effective tool for reaching your goal. It should be in regular use by most businesses.

12. Use telemarketing to boost your marketing campaigns

This may not be applicable to all businesses, but where appropriate, it can be used to take a marketing campaign to the next level. Think of the political campaigns. When the time is winding down and it's close to the election date, volunteers make an extra push by burning up the phone lines with calls for support. Perhaps you can try a version of this with your marketing campaign.

13. Publish a book or booklet

Copywriter Joe Vitale, president of Hypnotic Marketing Inc., has said that a book is one of the most powerful marketing tools around. Why? It provides you with fame, fortune, and immortality, he said. When you publish a book, you are perceived as an authority. Promotion of the book can result in speaking engagements and feature stories in newspapers and magazines. Other benefits are derived, especially free publicity, when you include your sales message inside the book. Should you feel you cannot write a full-length book, don't worry. You can write a booklet instead. Think in terms of a long how-to article or tip sheet. You may publish this as a brochure or as a booklet. Once published, you can offer it free to prospects or sell it directly. Once published, you may write up a press release about your "achievement" and send it to the appropriate media outlets.

14. Build a web site

This goes without saying. Every good business should have a web site. This is true whether your aim is to serve local or national clients, or whether you aim to sell directly or simply use the web as a publicity tool. (See Chapter 13, 15 Critical Facts about Using the Web.)

15. Open a discussion group along with your web site

As noted elsewhere in this book, creating a discussion group is an effective way to build customer loyalty and a thriving community base around your products and services. In addition to keeping in touch with your audience, the discussion group will allow you to know and understand their needs, wishes, problems, etc. What you learn in the group can aid you in developing or acquiring new products and services.

Creating a discussion group is an effective way to build customer loyalty and a thriving community base around your products and services.

16. Host an annual conference

This is another way to position yourself as a leader in your industry. Think of a weekend event with seminars, workshops, and refreshments that you can host in your hometown. Use your personal name or business name as the title of the event. Consider something like, "The First Annual Mary Doe Retail Conference," or "The First Annual Retail Success Conference."

Develop a few teaching ideas and invite other experts to participate. Promote the event locally through the Chamber of Commerce, local press, and of course, over the Internet. Encourage the speakers to submit press releases about their engagement to their hometown media.

You may also invite a public official to address the conference each year. This will almost certainly ensure press coverage.

17. Create a hot-line to provide quick tips about your service

Using a toll-free hot-line is a good way to serve your audience while standing out from the competition. Develop a series of daily how-to tips that your clients and prospects can access with a simple phone call. At the end of the message, include an offer and a call to action. Invite the listener to contact you for more information or for special discounts.

Once your hot-line is up and running, promote it aggressively through the local press. Don't forget to include newsletters, business cards, billing statements, and receipts, all of which are good vehicles for promoting your hot-line—and driving your sales message forward.

18. Hold a drawing for free giveaways

Although drawings are quite common for some retailers, a surprising number of them fail to do this on a regular basis. Neglecting to do this means you're missing out on a good opportunity to collect the names of your prospects and customers. In fact, collecting names is probably the biggest benefit. As noted above, once you have the names, you have a mailing list that you can use whenever you choose to.

While common among local store owners, drawings may also be used by other businesses. They can be held at a physical location or online. They are especially effective at speaking engagements where you can ask the audience to place their business cards in a hat (or box) and take a chance at winning a free gift.

19. Start a blog to share opinions and to interact with your audience

Today blogging is one of the most popular activities on the Internet. They're read by people on the local and national level. They're studied in schools and sometimes quoted by the national press. So far, they've proven to be an effective way to get the word out on a particular issue.

Perhaps you can start a blog that deals with both your personal life as well as your business topic. You can write daily or weekly. Use it to provide news, humor, or analysis of news reports. Whatever topic you choose to focus on, just remember to keep it friendly and personable. After all, you don't want to frighten off customers or prospects.

Although direct selling is generally not favorable in this forum, you may include a sig line at the bottom of each message.

And, as with the other tools described here, make every effort to promote your blog as often as you can. Encourage feedback from your readers. Listen to what they say. Then use what you learn to improve your products and services.

20. Become a business analyst for the local press

Assuming you are well-informed about your industry and you have all the right credentials, you can market yourself as an "expert on call" for the local press. Whenever they have an issue for which they need an expert opinion, they will call you for a "sound bite" to spice up their story.

Perhaps you've seen this done on the national level. Whenever there is a breaking story on a hot topic, the national media scramble for "talking heads"—experts who can talk on camera. Some of them are eventually hired as "analysts." Some recent examples are the many retired generals who comment on the Iraq war.

Well, you can follow their lead and become the preferred "analyst" in your community. Just put together a nice press kit that contains your photo, resume, cover letter, and any published articles. Call the local newspaper or TV station and let them know you are available for comments. Then send them your materials.

While you may or may not use all 20 of the ideas presented here, the important thing is to be creative, consistent, and aggressive in promoting your sales message on a regular basis. Only then will you reach the saturation point of marketing and have good visibility for your business.

Appendix A

Advertising Words That Command Attention

Act now
Advice to
Amazing
Announcing
At last
Available
Bargains
Be _____ (healthy, successful, popular, etc.)
Best
Better
Breakthrough
Call now
Closeout
Cope
Conquer
Crisis
Discover
Dollars (specific amount)

Do you
Dynamic
Easy
Enhance
Essential
Everything
Expert
Facts you
Fantastic
First
Free
Freedom
Get
Grow
Gain
Great
Guaranteed
Handle
Here's

How to

How much

How would

Incredible

Independence

Important

Improve

Life

Love

Magic

Make Money

New

Never

Now

Only

Opportunity

Over

Powerful

Profit

Proof

Protect

Quick

Receive

Revealing

Sale

Save

Secrets to

Special

Sex-appeal

Startling

Super

The truth of

This

Ultimate

Unique

Vital

Wanted

Yes

You

Appendix B

Arresting Advertising Headlines

T HE FOLLOWING HEADLINES WERE USED TO SUCCESSFULLY SELL PROD-
ucts and services. The list consists of copy for both consumer
and business-to-business advertisements. Some, you will notice,
are legendary in the advertising industry, having generated millions of dollars. Others listed here have run consistently (with
minor changes) for 10 to 40 years or more. Also included with each headline
is the name of the copywriter and/or organization that produced the copy.

With a little creativity, the concepts used for these successful headlines
can be adapted to fit your product or service. Experiment and see if you can
write similar copy. Then test it and measure the results.

Perhaps it's worth noting that this list is not intended to be exhaustive,
as there certainly are other types of headlines that can be used. The ones
mentioned here are given merely as examples and prompters to help you
brainstorm and develop copy for your own ads. That said, here's the list of
some of the most popular types of ads in use today.

1. Startling Statement Headlines

HOT!
A NEW CONSUMER CONCEPT LETS YOU BUY STOLEN MERCHANDISE
IF YOU'RE WILLING TO TAKE A RISK

—Joe Sugarman, JS&A National Sales Group

BREAKING NEWS—On March 1st 2004
NetExec@Work Has a New Home

2. News Headlines

LOCAL COMPANY PULLS YOU THROUGH THE HUSTLE AND BUSTLE OF
BUSY DAYS, USING STATE-OF-THE-ART EQUIPMENT

—Roscoe Barnes III for Glessner Communications

WE'RE LOOKING FOR PEOPLE TO WRITE
CHILDREN'S BOOKS

—Institute of Children's Literature

SECRETS OF THE MILLIONAIRES

—George Sterne

3. Question Headlines

IS THERE A WRITER IN YOU, TRYING TO GET OUT?

—Chapman University

WHAT WILL YOU DO WHEN THE IRS SUDDENLY WIPES
OUT YOUR CORPORATION'S TAX SHELTER BENEFITS?

—Ted Nicholas

CAN YOU PUT A PRICE TAG ON HAPPINESS?
TRY $5,195

—Hyundai

DO YOU KNOW THESE LOCAL VETERANS?

—Roscoe Barnes III for book, *Off to War*

ARE YOU TIRED OF WORKING FOR YOUR AD AGENCY?

—Pallace Inc.

IT'S 9 A.M. DO YOU KNOW WHERE YOUR EMPLOYEES ARE?
—Bureau of National Affairs

4. Clever Headlines

WHETHER YOU'RE RUNNING, SKIING, HIKING OR WRITING, IF YOU USE
***GORE-TEX*® FABRIC CORRECTLY, WE'LL ALL FEEL COMFORTABLE**
—W.L. Gore & Associates Inc.

HOW TO WIN CLIENTS AND INFLUENCE PROFITS
—Roscoe Barnes III for ATX/Kleinrock

IS YOUR MARKETING LIKE A SÉANCE?

WE MAY BE CRAZY FOR GIVING
ALL THIS AWAY FOR ONLY $500 ...
But then we've always been crazy for our customers
—Roscoe Barnes for Total Kleinrock Office by ATX/Kleinrock

5. Problem Statement Headline

TO THE PERSON WHO WANTS RELIEF FROM HEARTBURN
AND OTHER DIGESTIVE PROBLEMS ...
—Roscoe Barnes III for Gastroenterology Associates

NO MORE REJECTION!
—Don Massey

"JUST ONE DROP DID IT"
Scientists accidentally create miracle pain eraser ...
—SoothanolX2 from NorthStar Nutritionals

6. Command Headlines

NOW TRY ONE OF THE WORLD'S MOST ADVANCED
HEARING AIDS ... RISK FREE!
—EXCEL Hearing Solutions

STOP TAKING VITAMINS
—Joe Sugarman, JS&A National Sales Group

121

SPEAK SPANISH LIKE A DIPLOMAT!

—Audio Forum

STOP BURNING PROFITS

—Sylvania

IMPRESS EDITORS!

—Writer's Digest Books

7. Benefit and Promise Headlines

HOW TO PUBLISH YOUR BOOK

—Carlton Press

FREE $10 BOOK

—Russ von Hoelscher

HOW TO GET ENTHUSIASTIC APPLAUSE—EVEN A STANDING OVATION—EVERYTIME YOU SPEAK

—Ted Nicholas

$500 A DAY WRITER'S UTOPIA

—Jerry Buchanan

HOW TO GET RICH IN MAIL ORDER

—Melvin Powers

LINK 8 PCs TO YOUR MAINFRAME ONLY $2,395

—Winterhalter Inc.

YOU CAN MAKE A FISTFUL OF DOLLARS WITH A FEW LITTLE SKETCHES!

—Roscoe Barnes III

HOW TO WAKE UP THE FINANCIAL GENIUS INSIDE OF YOU

—Mark O. Haroldsen

FIND HARD DISK FILES FAST!

—Polaris Software

THE LAZY MAN'S WAY TO RICHES

—Joe Karbo

8. Testimonial Headlines

"SCRIPT WRITING HAS NEVER BEEN FASTER OR EASIER!"

—Cinovation Inc.®

"I TOOK THE PICTURE AND WAS SET FOR LIFE."

—Jeff Peters

"NO MORE GLASSES AND WE LOVE IT!"

—Gladsden Refractive Center

**THEY LAUGHED WHEN I SAT DOWN AT THE PIANO,
BUT WHEN I STARTED TO PLAY …**

—John Caples

"I CAN HELP YOU MAKE THE RIGHT MOVE."
—Deborah Sanders of Coldwell Banker Bigham, REALTORS®

9. Reason Why Headlines

**THIRTEEN REASONS TO LET U.S.A. DIRECT QUOTE
YOUR NEXT DIRECT MAIL PACKAGE**

—U.S.A. Direct Inc.

**7 REASONS TO LOCATE YOUR
EUROPEAN CALL CENTER IN BELGIUM**

—Belgacom North America

SIX QUESTIONS TO ASK BEFORE HIRING A FREELANCE COPYWRITER

—Clifton Parker

Appendix C

Bibliography/
Recommended Reading

Adams, Charles F. *Common Sense in Advertising*. New York: McGraw-Hill, 1965.

Antin, Brad H. and Alan J. Antin. *Secrets from the Lost Art of Common Sense Marketing*. Clearwater, FL: The Antin Marketing Group, 1992.

Barnes III, Roscoe. *Big Bucks from Little Sketches*. Gettysburg, PA: McKinley & Henson, 1993.

_____. *Discover Your Talent and Find Fulfillment*. Gettysburg, PA: McKinley & Henson, 1992.

_____. *Secrets of a Writing Hustler*. Kandiyohi, MN: Filbert Publishing, 2004.

_____. *The Guide to Effective Gospel Tract Ministry*. Elkton, MD: Church Growth Institute, 2004.

Bayan, Richard. *Words that Sell*. Lincolnwood, IL: Contemporary Books, 1984.

Bly, Robert W. *Ads that Sell*. Brentwood, New York: Asher-Gallant Press, 1988.

_____. *The Copywriter's Handbook*. New York: Henry Holt & Co., 1985.

Blake, Gary and Robert W. Bly. *The Elements of Copywriting*. New York: Macmillan, 1997.

Bodian, Nat G. *Direct Marketing Rules of Thumb*. New York: McGraw-Hill Inc., 1995.

_____. *How to Choose a Winning Title*. Phoenix, AZ: The Oryx Press, 1989.

Benson, Richard V. *Secrets of Successful Direct Mail*. Lincolnwood, IL: NTC Business Books, 1989.

Bovee, Cortland L. and William F. Arens. *Contemporary Advertising*. Homewood, IL: Richard D. Irwin Inc., 1982.

Bowerman, Peter. *The Well-Fed Writer*. Atlanta, GA: Fanove Publishing, 2000.

Caples, John. *How to Make Your Advertising Make Money*. Englewood Cliffs, NJ: Prentice-Hall, 1983.

_____. *Tested Advertising Methods*. Englewood Cliffs, NJ: Prentice-Hall, 1974.

Ferdi, Liz. *Successful Direct Mail*. Hauppauge, NY: Barron's Educational Series Inc., 1997.

Gauss, Chester A. and Lucius I. Wightman. *Practical Business Administration, Vol. III, Advertising*. Chicago: American Technical Society, 1935.

Glim, Aesop. *Copy—The Core of Advertising*. New York: McGraw-Hill, 1949.

Gosden Jr., Freeman F. *Direct Marketing Success*. New York: John Wiley & Sons, 1985.

Hahn, Fred E. *Do-It-Yourself Advertising*. New York: John Wiley & Sons Inc., 1993.

Hicks, Tyler G. *Mail Order Success Secrets*. Rocklin, CA: Prima Publishing, 1992.

Hoelscher, Russ von. *How You Can Make a Fortune Selling Information by Mail*. San Diego: Profit Ideas, 1988.

Hopkins, Claude C. *My Life in Advertising & Scientific Advertising*. Lincolnwood, IL: NTC Business Books, 1995.

Howard, Lee. *$50,000 a Year from Mail Order Ads*. Forth Worth, TX: Premier Publishers, 1988.

_____. *Mail Order Success Secrets*. Clearwater, FL: Selective Books Inc., 1994.

Kalian, Robert. *Mail Order Success Secrets*. White Plains, NY: Roblin Press, 1998.

Kennedy, Daniel S. *The Ultimate Marketing Plan*. Holbrook, MA: Adams Media Corp., 2000.

_____. *The Ultimate Sales Letter*. Holbrook, MA: Bob Adams Inc., 1990.

Kleppner, Otto, Russell Thomas and Glenn Verrill. *Otto Kleppner's Advertising Procedure*, 8th Ed., Englewood Cliffs, NJ: Prentice-Hall Inc., 1983.

Lant, Jeffrey, Ph.D. *Cash Copy*. Cambridge: JLA Publications, 1989.

Levinson, Jay Conrad. *Guerrilla Advertising*. Boston: Houghton Mifflin Co., 1994.

Lewis, Gordon Herschell. *Direct Mail Copy that Sells*. Englewood Cliffs, NJ: Prentice Hall Inc., 1984.

_____. *On the Art of Writing Copy*, 3d Ed., Racom Communications, 2003.

_____. *Sales Letters that Sizzle*, 2d Ed., Chicago, IL: NTC Business Books, 1999.

Margolis, Charles. *How to Write Copy that Sells*. Cleveland, OH: Speedibooks, 1987.

Nicholas, Ted. *Magic Words that Bring You Riches*. Indian Rocks Beach, FL: Nicholas Direct Inc., 1995.

Ogilvy, David. *Confessions of an Advertising Man*. New York: Macmillan, 1987.

_____. *Ogilvy on Advertising*. New York: Vintage, 1985.

Perrin, Carl. *So You Want to Be a Writer*. Auburn, CA: eBookstand Books, 2002.

Powers, Melvin. *How to Get Rich in Mail Order*. No. Hollywood, CA: Wilshire Book Company, 1998.

Provost, Gary. *100 Ways to Improve Your Writing*. New York: New American Library, 1985.

Rohrer, Norman B. *Discover Your Possibilities in Writing*. Hume Lake, CA: Christian Writers Guild, 1992.

Roman, Kenneth and Jane Maas. *How to Advertise*, 2d Ed., New York: St. Martin's Griffin, 1992.

Reecher, David A. and Jerry Buchanan. *Maxwell Sackheim's Billion Dollar Marketing Concepts and Applications*. Vancouver, WA: TOWERS Club USA Press, 1966.

Safire, William and Leonard Sifir. *Good Advice on Writing*. New York, Simon & Schuster, 1992.

Sackheim, Maxwell. *How to Advertise Yourself*. New York: Macmillan, 1978.

Schwab, Victor. *How to Write a Good Advertisement*. Hollywood, CA: Wilshire, 1962.

Schwartz, Eugene M. *Breakthrough Advertising*. New York: Boardroom Books, 1984.

Scott, Dewitt H. *Secrets of Successful Writing*. Harrisonburg, VA: Christian Light Publications, 1998.

Strunk Jr., William and E.B. White. *The Elements of Style*, 4th Ed., New York: Longman, 2000.

Stilson, Galen. *59 Response/Profit Tips, Tricks & Techniques*. Fort Worth, TX: Premier Publishers Inc., 1997.

_____. *How to Make the Successful Transition from Small-Time to Big-Time Mail Order ... on a Limited Budget*. Fort Worth, TX: Premier Publishers Inc., 1996.

_____. *How to Write and Design Money-Making Response Advertisements*. Fort Worth, TX: Premier Publishers Inc., 1997.

_____. *How You Can Write Winning Sales Letters*. Fort Worth, TX: Premier Publishers Inc., 1998.

_____. *The Success How-to's of Money-Making Direct Mail*. Fort Worth, TX: Premier Publishers Inc., 1998.

Sugarman, Joseph. *Marketing Secrets of a Mail Order Maverick*. Las Vegas, NV: DelStar Books, 1998.

Tighe, John Francis. *Making Money with Mail*. Wellfleet, MA: PMT Press, 1993.

Vitale, Joe. *Cyber Writing*. New York: AMACOM, 1997.

_____. *The AMA Complete Guide to Small Business Advertising*. Lincolnwood, IL: NTC Business Books, 1995.

_____. *There's a Customer Born Every Minute*. New York: AMACOM, 1998.

_____. *The Seven Lost Secrets of Success*. Awareness Publications.

Watkins, Julian Lewis. *The 100 Greatest Advertisements*. Toronto, Canada: Coles Publishing Co. Ltd., 1959.

Zinsser, William. *On Writing Well*, 5th Ed., New York: HaperCollins Publishers, 1994.

Appendix D

Recommended Periodicals

Advertising Age
711 Third Ave.
New York, NY 10017
Phone: 212-210-0100
www.adage.com

Adweek
770 Broadway
New York, NY 10003
Phone: 646-654-5421
www.adweek.com

B-to-B
360 N. Michigan Ave.
Chicago, IL 60601
www.btobonline.com

Direct
http://directmag.com

Direct Marketing
224 Seventh St.
Garden City, NY 11530
Phone: 516-746-6700
www.dmcny.org

DM News
100 Avenue of the Americas
New York, NY 10013
Phone: 212-925-7300
www.dmnews.com

Entrepreneur Magazine
Phone: 800-274-6229
www.entrepreneur.com

FundRaising Success
1500 Spring Garden St., Suite 1200
Philadelphia, PA 19130
Phone: 215-238-5300

Home Business Magazine
Phone: 714-968-0331
www.homebusinessmag.com

Inside Direct Mail
1500 Spring Garden St., Suite 1200
Philadelphia, PA 19130-4094

Money Making Opportunities
Success Publishing International
11071 Ventura Blvd.
Studio City, CA 91604
Phone: 818-980-9166

Public Relations Journal
33 Maiden Lane, 11th Flr.
New York, NY 10038
Phone: 212-460-1400
www.prsa.org

Sales and Marketing Management
770 Broadway 7th Flr.
New York, NY 10003
Phone: 800-641-2030
www.salesandmarketing.com

Target Marketing
1500 Spring Garden St., Suite 1200
Philadelphia, PA 19130
Phone: 215-238-5300
www.targetonline.com

The Tidal Wave Business NewsMagazine
9400 Snowden River Pkwy.
Suite #110 - PMB #281
Columbia, MD 21045
Phone: 877-660-3175
www.kineticwavellc.com

Writers Journal
P.O. Box 394
Perham, MN 56573
Phone: 218-346-7921
www.writersjournal.com

Appendix E

Recommended Online Newsletters

THERE ARE MANY ONLINE MAGAZINES/NEWSLETTERS/E-ZINES THAT provide practical, easy-to-use tips on various aspects of marketing, writing, and advertising. Those listed below are just a few of the many that should prove helpful in crafting effective direct response advertising copy.

Audacious Marketing Mastery by Deborah McLaughlin & Juanita Bellavance
www.audaciousmarketingmastery.com

Bencivenga's Bullets
www.bencivengabullets.com

The Book Coach Says by Judy Cullins
www.bookcoaching.com

Booklet Tips by Paulette
www.tipsbooklets.com

B-to-B Marketing Online
www.btobonline.com

The Direct Response Letter
www.bly.com

The E-zine Queen's Publish for Profits
www.ezinequeen.com

Excess Voice
www.nickusborne.com/excess-voice.htm

Early to Rise
www.earlytorise.com

The Golden Thread Online
www.awaionline.com/thegoldenthread/index.php

The Health Care Marketing Connection newsletter by Kelly Robbins
www.kellyrobbinsllc.com

Joe Robson's Copywriter's Digest
www.adcopywriting.com/Newsletter_Subsc.htm

John Forde's Copywriters' Roundtable
www.jackforde.com

Marketing Minute
www.yudkin.com/markmin.htm

The MarketSmart Newsletter
www.bookmarketingprofits.com/page4.html

Money the Write Way
www.moneythewriteway.com

News You Can Use by Joe Vitale
www.mrfire.com

Dr Nunley's Marketing Newsletter
http://drnunley.com/newsletter.htm

Paul Hartunian's Million-Dollar Publicity Strategies
www.prprofits.com

Publishing Poynters by Dan Poynter
www.parapublishing.com

Quick Tips from Marketing Mentor by Ilise Benun
www.marketing-mentor.com/html/tips.html

Dr. Ralph Wilson's Web Marketing Today
www.wilsonweb.com

The Success Margin
www.tednicholas.com

Target Marketing Tipline
www.targetmarketingmag.com

Tips & Updates from Writer's Digest
www.writersdigest.com

The Total Package by Clayton Makepeace
www.makepeacetotalpackage.com

The Well-Fed Writer by Peter Bowerman
www.wellfedwriter.com

The Web Marketing Advisor by Daniel Levis
www.web-marketingadvisor.com

Writing Etc.
www.filbertpublishing.com

Writing for Dollars
www.writingfordollars.com

WritersWeekly Newsletter
www.writersweekly.com

Appendix F

Recommended Bloggers and Other Online Sources

1. Bloggers

This list consists of professional copywriters, authors, and publishers.

Angela Adair-Hoy
www.writersweekly.com

Bob Bly
www.bly.com

Beth Erickson
www.filbertpublishing.com

Clayton Makepeace
www.makepeacetotalpackage.com

Denny Hatch's Business Common Sense
www.targetmarketingmag.com

Dianne Huff's B-2-B Marketing
http://www.marcom-writer-blog.com/

Ilise Benun
http://www.marketing-mentor.com

Joe Vitale
www.mrfire.com

John Kremer on Marketing
www.publishersmarketplace.com/members/JohnKremer/

Judy Cullins
www.bookcoaching.com

Kelly Robbins
www.kellyrobbinsllc.com

Marcia Yudkin
www.yudkin.com/markmin.htm

M.J. Rose's Buzz, Balls & Hype
www.publishersmarketplace.com/members/BkDoctorSin/

Paulette Ensign
www.tipsbooklets.com

Peter Bowerman
www.wellfedwriter.com

Richard Armstrong
http://richardarmstrong.blogspot.com/

2. Discussion Groups

Although most of these groups focus on the general aspects of writing for publication, some include business professionals who offer tips and advice on copywriting. One in particular (AWAI) has students who post questions about all areas of copywriting.

AbsoluteWrite
www.absolutewrite.com
Provides a forum with advice on types of writing issues, including copywriting and writing for publication.

American Writers and Artists Institute (AWAI)
www.awaionline.com
Provides detailed and enlightening discussion on all aspects of commercial writing.

Angela Adair-Hoy's Group

www.writersweekly.com

Provides forum for discussion on writing and publishing, as well as advice for determining legitimate publishers.

Beth Erickson and Vicky Heron's Group

http://finance.groups.yahoo.com/group/CopywriterMastermind/ Or www.filbertpublishing.com

Provides detailed question and answers with practical advice for copywriting and self-promotion.

www.writers.net

Provides listing of agents, authors, editors, publishers, and discussion forum for all aspects of writing and publishing.

3. Web sites

American Writers and Artists Institute (AWAI)

www.awaionline.com

Provides home-study course, conferences and helpful discussion forum.

Bob Bly

www.bly.com

Provides scores of free articles on types of writing along with useful listings of vendors and other resources.

Entrepreneur

www.entrepreneur.com

Provides ezines, articles, books and everything you ever wanted to know about starting and running a successful business.

Joe Vitale

www.mrfire.com

Provides tons of free articles with advice on copywriting and publicity.

Monthly Copywriting Genius

www.monthlycopywritinggenius.com

Provides interviews with copywriters and frequent reviews of sucessful promotions.

The Small Business Advocate

www.smallbusinessadvocate.com

Provides a radio show and website with practical information for small businesses.

Index